IRONY IN THE SHORT STORIES
OF EDITH WHARTON

IRONY IN THE SHORT STORIES OF EDITH WHARTON

Charlee M. Sterling

The Edwin Mellen Press
Lewiston•Queenston•Lampeter

Library of Congress Cataloging-in-Publication Data

Sterling, Charlee M.
   Irony in the short stories of Edith Wharton / Charlee M. Sterling.
     p. cm.
   Includes bibliographical references and index.
   ISBN 0-7734-5984-7
   1. Wharton, Edith, 1862-1937--Technique. 2. Narration (Rhetoric)--History--20th
century. 3. Point-of-view (Literature) 4. Irony in literature. 5. Short story. I. Title.

PS3545.H16Z8785 2005
813'.52--dc22

2005049617

hors série.

A CIP catalog record for this book is available from the British Library.

Front cover photo: Edith Wharton's home, The Mount, in Lenox, Massachusetts

The Edwin Mellen Press
Box 450
Lewiston, New York
USA 14092-0450

The Edwin Mellen Press
Box 67
Queenston, Ontario
CANADA L0S 1L0

The Edwin Mellen Press, Ltd.
Lampeter, Ceredigion, Wales
UNITED KINGDOM SA48 8LT

Printed in the United States of America

To my family.

Table of Contents

Preface

It is a pleasure to welcome Charlee Sterling's study of irony in Edith Wharton's short stories to the collection of Wharton criticism. In her memoir, *A Backward Glance,* Wharton records her earliest recollection of a winter walk on Fifth Avenue with her father and attributes her awakening to "conscious life," ironically, to the "two tremendous forces of love and vanity" that she encountered on this walk (3). However, it was the publication over thirty years later of her first collection of stories, *The Greater Inclination*, which, she says sincerely, "called her soul to life" and finally gave her entry as a citizen into the "Land of Letters" (119). A successful writer, Wharton searches through her memories of the "prosaic" goodness of her respectable ancestors for stories that might have inspired her "childish fancy" (23) and set her on her career as a writer. She reports she does not recall "a time when [she] did not want to 'make up' stories" (33), and though these earliest tales were not recorded, she remembers they were always about "real people" caught in the "daily coil of 'things that might have happened'" (43). It was always the "real" that inspired her—whether the "domestic dramas" of the Greek gods or the whispered insinuations about her cousin George Alfred (33, 24). Wharton's awareness of the contradictions of her life and her fascination with the ironies of life in general, as well as her ability to capture these subtleties, still intrigue her readers today.

We know Edith Wharton as a writer of novels—she wrote twenty-five. She also wrote essays, travel books, criticism and reviews, and a vast correspondence with writers and important figures of her time. Although she won her greatest popular and critical successes with her novels, she never gave up writing short stories, completing eighty-six over the course of her career. By her report, subjects swarmed about her "like mosquitoes" (*Backward Glance* 199). Charlee Sterling has selected a number of stories from this swarm to study in depth. In so doing, she not only provides readers with insight into the individual stories she discusses but also develops a basis for analyzing Wharton's use of irony in all her fiction. As Sterling points out, Wharton's stories have been largely neglected by critics. Nor, although readers have long noted her irony, have critics given this complex strategy the attention it warrants. Sterling's study fills in these missing pieces in Wharton criticism.

Focusing on Wharton's narrative strategies and building on formal definitions of layered irony developed by D.C. Muecke in *The Compass of Irony* and the range of overt and covert, stable and unstable, ironies elucidated by Wayne C. Booth in *The Rhetoric of Fiction,* as well as contributions from other critics, Sterling draws a careful and convincing picture of the range of Wharton's use of irony. She finds Wharton more experimental and modern than some dismissive critics allow, and she finds the source of optimism in much of Wharton's work in her ability to use various levels of narrative distancing to sustain open-ended ambiguities in her stories. We all sense Wharton's irony, but Sterling gives us the vocabulary to perceive and distinguish its subtleties.

Sterling's book with its many examples and detailed analyses of a manageable list of stories will give readers familiar with Wharton's stories access to the subtle use of irony in these tales; equally Sterling's study will send readers who have concentrated on Wharton's novels back, with renewed interest and appreciation, to her short stories. Wharton reported that she, like all writers, wanted to discover "authentic human nature" (*Backward Glance* 127). Ultimately Sterling's study convinces us that Wharton, through her skilled manipulation of the relationship between narrator, characters, and audience, more often than not, succeeded in this aim. Wharton's genius as an ironist and as a story writer, put forth by Sterling, further secures a place for her short stories in the canon of American literature and on the reading tables of those who like a good read.

Carol B. Sapora

Carol B. Sapora is Professor of Language and Literature at Villa Julie College, Stevenson, Maryland.

Acknowledgments

I would like to thank Ross Posnock, for taking me on sight unseen, and for reading my work when I had despaired that anyone ever would. I am grateful for the insights and suggestions of Josephine Hendin and Cyrus Patell, whose comments and reflections were invaluable.

Thank you also to my colleagues Carol Maccini, Judith McFadden and Roger Bridges, who calmed me, consoled me, and who continually offered me their support, suggestions, and astute judgments, and especially my department chair and fellow Wharton scholar, Carol Sapora, who so patiently read and thoughtfully commented on my work, and whose fresh and frank opinions always kept me interested in my subject.

Introduction

When we think about the major American short story writers of the twentieth century, the names Henry James, Ernest Hemingway, and of course later writers such as John Updike and Raymond Carver may come to mind. But many tend to leave off one of the most prolific, popular, and underrated short story writers of the early part of the century: Edith Wharton. Even today, after attempts by feminist critics to claim her as their own, Wharton's short stories have only just begun to receive the serious scrutiny they merit. We might today encounter Wharton's name in popular magazines such as *Vogue*; as Dale M. Bauer points out in the preface to a study on Wharton's later works, she might even be mentioned in a *New Yorker* cartoon, or in a *New York Times* article.[1] Several of Wharton's novels have become the darlings of the television and film industry, but her name is synonymous with the ideal of a past stable social order, a caretaker or a preserver of tradition, as earlier critics suggest Bauer xv); that she is popular again now reveals that we continue to see her as "an icon of a by-gone era rather than as a writer devoted to the most pressing problems of her day" (Bauer xv).

Why does this continue to be so? After all, only a handful of her novels are read or taught: *The House of Mirth, Ethan Frome, The Age of Innocence*. Many do not realize that Wharton wrote many essays, poetry, and other novels that, though widely read in her day, now have little readership, let alone critical attention. Furthermore, Wharton was the author of eighty-six short stories over the span of her career, many of which today are still obscure because they are often neglected, misread or poorly interpreted. Is Wharton, then, merely a Jamesian imitator and an atavism? Perhaps; perhaps not. But we can truly judge the

---

[1] This is from a *New York Times*, November 17, 1993 article on women's power lunches (Bauer, xv).

importance of Wharton's works and her contribution to American letters by including serious attention to the canon of Wharton's short stories, and not just to the few that are frequently anthologized.

With twelve or so exceptions, the greater part of Wharton's extensive short story canon is unexplored, though they are readily accessible for casual readers and scholars alike, both from R.W.B. Lewis' and Anita Brookner's editions of Wharton's short fiction, and from numerous websites with links to the individual texts. The number of critical biographies discussing the short fiction, as well as Lewis' definitive and complete edition of Wharton's stories, has done much to boost readership; in his introduction to the short fiction Lewis points out their importance – that it is in the short stories that Wharton sought "the truth of human experience: it was where she tested the limits of human freedom and found the terms to define the human mystery" (157). Further, Margaret McDowell, also a pioneer in bringing Wharton's short stories to more general recognition, devotes a chapter of her book *Edith Wharton* to the short stories. McDowell discusses both Wharton's theory of fiction as outlined in *The Writing of Fiction* and her practices by briefly examining individual stories. McDowell concludes that "her best tales reveal extraordinary psychological and moral insight," reinforcing Lewis' praise for the depth with which Wharton deals with "human situations" (85). McDowell is also one of the few critics to assert that Wharton produced some of her best work after, not before, 1920, and particularly in the arena of short fiction: "she may have reached the peak of her skill in the 1920s and 1930s, a fact that argues against the assumption that her creativity waned after *The Age of Innocence*" (86).

Much of the current short story criticism is directed towards feminist themes, and towards her ghost stories, which, says Sandra Gilbert, give Wharton a medium for "saying the unsayable" (qutd. In White 164). Van Wyck Brooks and Grace Kellogg further assert that perhaps the short fiction, and not the novel, is Wharton at her best. But little has been done to prove this assertion.

Despite these praises, the pervasive critical attitude towards the short stories has been that they are not worthy of much critical attention. Wharton's lack of innovation in the genre and her lack of experimentation with form are cited; they mention her emphasis on situation and reliance on coincidence at the expense of characterization, her cold, detached relationship with readers and characters alike, her literary elitism, her often enigmatic messages, and the pessimism her short fiction contains. In response to the Lewis edition, Louis Kronenberger commented that although Wharton's stories are occasionally "astute and mature," most are "trivial and merely entertaining," and "contribute nothing to the enlargement of literature" (99-100). Lawrence J. Dessner, furthermore, found that although the short stories themselves can be clever, Wharton's "tendency to use a short story form as the underlying form of a novel" weakens even her best:

> It is the tendency to take delight in a complex situation and in the intricate plot manipulations it makes possible, and to create characters whose prime function is not to think, to wonder, to discover, but to be manipulated by, and to demonstrate, the author's ingenuity. Neither protagonist nor reader is allowed wider scope. (60)

These assessments hardly do justice to Wharton's short stories; what does she contribute to the form – what is the brilliance of her craft that would merit more than simply inclusion in the mainstream of the American short story canon?

To understand the genius of Wharton's art we must consider the literary circumstances in which she was writing. Wharton first published a short story ("Mrs. Mansey's View") in 1890, just as the American literary scene was in great flux. The romantic idealism of Emerson and Whitman was in decline, disintegrating into the sentimental, the sensational, the morally idealistic and pseudo-romantic. Ever rising in popularity was a proliferation of magazine fiction, through which many women gained financial success, as well as the sentimental novel, which Wharton saw her mother and other female adults reading, but was never herself allowed to read. America's elite writers responded to the dissolution of idealism in many ways: Howells with his brand of realism, Twain with humor and satire, Norris and others with deterministic naturalism, and later writers with the modernist experiment bent on divorcing itself from nineteenth-century America's literary past altogether. How did Wharton respond: with a turn from the "ideal" to the "real," or with a turn towards the forces of heredity and environment as determinants of human character? Or did she turn inwards towards the self and towards modern despair?

Wharton tacitly explores ideas similar to those of her immediate predecessors and her contemporaries in her short stories: the overwhelming density of modern life, the sense of social wastelands in which few meaningful and lasting human relationships form, and the increasing contempt for the commercialization of social relationships and of art. Ultimately Wharton sees the possibilities of life reduced by cultural and social pressures; some of the short stories she wrote towards the end of her life read like a sophisticated Dreiserian abstract on cultural determinism. Though much attention has been paid to her ghost stories, in some sense all of Wharton's stories are ghost stories; characters never fully reconcile their external obligations with their internal desires, choosing to live by one or the other exclusively, haunted by the path they have disregarded.

However, just as we certainly cannot label Wharton a modernist, we must be careful about labeling her a naturalist. Though Wharton in *A Backward Glance* claims Darwin as one of her "awakeners," she is at most a soft determinist who, while not denying the existence or importance of free will, undermines it even as she identifies it, responding more with irony than with determinism or despair. We cannot submerge the body of Wharton's work within one literary period, therefore, because she exploits any elements and techniques that are available, as suits a particular situation or group of characters. In reaction to the moral idealism and sentimentalism of the middle and end of the nineteenth century, Wharton creates a fiction in touch with, but distinct from that of her predecessors, contemporaries and immediate successors. Wharton frequently identifies themes, characters and their ideals, and then undercuts them with an ironic method that is the center of her genius. As Carol Miller points out in her essay on irony in *The House of Mirth,* Wharton's "deserved identification as an ironist" is one of several "obstacle[es] to an objective evaluation of her work because of the neo-oral, anti-ironic preferences of structuralism, whose theorists have[…]tended to devalue irony on the ground that it creates alienation which divorces writer and audience and fragments the effectual power of the text" (82). Miller, however, correctly identifies Wharton's view of human experience as ironic, and not entirely determinist: Wharton's aesthetic sensibility is at times romantic, especially with her focus on and favoring of the individual and his or her free will despite the forces of heredity and environment seeking to undermine it (85-86).

Dale M. Bauer points out in *Edith Wharton's Brave New Politics* (1994) that it is Wharton's ability to be both ironic and sympathetic towards her characters that is central to her artistic vision; irony and sympathy are "the twin features of her imagination throughout her career, and in her loneliness, they also marked her response to a world irrevocably changed" (165). Furthermore, Carol Singley's study on Wharton and her spiritual quest suggests that for Wharton, the only appropriate response towards late nineteenth-century sentimentality is irony (10); this vision is modernist, not Victorian, refusing nostalgia, and rejecting easy explanations for difficult moral or spiritual dilemmas (24).

Irony, then, is the genius of Edith Wharton's short stories: she has a dual vision of irony and sympathy towards her characters in the short stories that creates a "fictive reality" in which some of her characters, as well as her readers, temporarily believe, and an "authentic reality" of which her readers, and if they are fortunate, her characters too catch a glimpse. Her countering of realistic, deterministic and romantic elements stylistically and thematically within the text of her short stories is one way Wharton creates irony, as Carol Miller asserts, and is itself the justification for its use: irony is Wharton's aesthetic response to the literary methods and ideas of her immediate predecessors and contemporaries, and the audiences they draw (83).

However, the *degree* of irony – the sharpness of its effect on the reader – depends upon the ironic perspective Wharton chooses for each story. Wharton achieves different degrees of ironic effect by varying point of view. Thus every story is not the same story, every narrator is not the cold, detached and sarcastic narrator with which Wharton has come to be associated. Wharton manipulates the fictive "authenticity" of her characters' responses to their situations by manipulating point of view, and therefore controls the pitch of the ironic effect upon her readers. Wharton generates three modes of irony from three types of narrators. First, her use of a third-person omniscient narrator who acts, to use June Howard's terms, as the detached and uninvolved "observer" to undercut ironically her characters' perspective, is perhaps the most conventional ironic method Wharton employs. A more sophisticated, more highly-pitched irony stems from Wharton's use of a "spectator" narrator, a first-person narrator marginally concerned in, but not utterly dependent on, the outcome of events. But perhaps the most poignant and subtle irony that Wharton generates in the short stories is through her dispensing with the "observer" and "spectator" narrator altogether, instead relying on the interplay between "fictive reality" as created by dialogue and by compressed symbolism of the setting, and the "authentic" psychological reality of the protagonist, a central consciousness whose mind we have access to through Wharton's use of interior monologue. Some of her very best stories rely on characters that utterly misread, misinterpret or refuse to recognize their own situations, but with whom we, submerged within the minds of such characters, are forced to sympathize despite our awareness of their misinterpretation.

While most of the critical focus on Wharton has been on a few of the twenty novels, and on only a handful of the short stories, including the ghost stories, and stories such as "The Potboiler," "Souls Belated," and "Roman Fever," there has recently been a renewed interest in Wharton's other work. This interest takes the form of several articles on various short stories, book chapters, and even two full-length studies of the short stories.

Dale M. Bauer's *Edith Wharton's Brave New Politics*, for example, published in 1994, is a good example of criticism that focuses on the less-well-known work. Bauer argues that the second half of Wharton's career differs from the first half in that in the second half, Wharton is less concerned with the formalist issues of her craft, and more interested in "the politics of culture" (xi). Such meta-concerns about state of culture and the future of the world she knows links her to another literary group explicitly sharing and writing about such concerns: Sinclair Lewis calls them the "three new young Americans"— Hemingway, Thomas Wolfe, and William Faulkner, who represent a new kind of writing with a new set of ideas (xi).[2] Although outwardly Wharton had no interest in writing about politics, she too is interested in the status of politics in literature (xi). Bauer's study, therefore, examines the later works, from *Summer*, published in 1917, through Wharton's death in 1937, in order to interpret and understand these works in relation to such political issues (xii). Bauer frequently discusses these works from the point of view of feminist theory, asking why women ally themselves with the "communities" they do – a recurring question in feminist theory (3).

The latter part of Wharton's career, Bauer points out, has up until this point received less critical scrutiny, based on the assessments of critics such as Percy Lubbock and R.W. B. Lewis, who both dismiss as weak much of what Wharton wrote after 1920 (xii). Their criticism has shaped critical response to her later works through this century (xii). But like Candace Waid, who in her

---

[2] This is from a June 1931 letter to Wharton from Sinclair Lewis (Bauer xi).

8

discussion of *Ghosts,* comments that some of these late short stories are her best, or even more recently still, like Helen Killoran, who asserts that viewing Wharton's later work as weak is a "mistake," Bauer also suggests that the works from the second half of Wharton's career are not focused upon because of the politicizing of both conservative and feminist critics (Waid 175; Killoran 4; Bauer xii). But for Wharton, Bauer argues, an earlier concern with form becomes a late interest and "immersion" in "mass culture," though "no less brilliantly achieved" (xii):

> Wharton was seldom interested in dedicating her fiction to social problems, or in reflecting a specific reality, since she distrusted the ability of "the big 'intelligent public'" to recognize the complexity of the relation between political reform and narrative resolution . . . By presenting these problems — of reproductive choice, personal affiliations, and political allegiance— in dialogue with each other and through internal and social debates, Wharton offered her own reconstructed social scene, relying much more than before on the mass culture around her to explore the intricacy of her own antimodernism. (xii)

Bauer sees the later works as interesting not merely because they are Wharton's and therefore validate the excellence of her earlier achievement, but because they reveal a Wharton aching for even more public recognition, and an even broader audience, especially as this and her concern for marketing herself successfully takes her farther and farther away from the detested "lady novelist" that so many have called her (xiii). Bauer's goal in this study is to examine the works that span this time period in order to reveal how Wharton's later "purposes" changed: examining the problems in intimate relationships brought on by politics and culture, and "how Wharton's narratives arrange and attempt to resolve her own cultural fears and ambivalence" (xiv).

Although the majority of Bauer's study focuses on the late novels *Summer*, *A Mother's Recompense*, *Twilight Sleep*, *The Children*, and the posthumous *The Buccaneers*, she devotes one complete chapter to the short story

"Roman Fever." In the introduction, Bauer mentions that in this short story, as well as in others such as "The Other Two," and "Autres Temps . . ." Wharton explores the theme of daughters' "dark inheritance" from mothers, entering into questions about the nature of inheritance itself (8). In these stories and in some of the longer works too, Wharton challenges the meaning of racial and gender categories, entering into the popular public discussions begun during the Reconstruction debates about biologically based racism and sexism, and eugenics (8).

Bauer's study concludes by investigating briefly Wharton's self-declared ironic stance as "Edith Agonistes," fighting to save the "inner life" – her self-description that appears as the signature of a letter (Bauer 165).[3] Wharton, at this point in her life, envisions herself to be the sole warrior against cultural forces threatening the "inner life" (5). Her vision is dual – one aspect of it is a denial that the American self or culture is fixed and unchangeable (5); another aspect of this vision is to see the role of fiction as instructive: changing how we identify with cultural icons by presenting characters who develop alternative values for "new cultural situations," or who do or do not to varying degrees of success (5). By creating a new way for readers to understand and identify with characters – with sympathy – we might understand the difficulty for those "who are bewildered about and [are] struggling to find niches in modernity" (6). Wharton uses the rhetoric, terminology and "idiom" of mass culture to find a means of understanding and challenging the world in which she found herself, rather than clinging to a world which would never return, or perhaps, never even existed. As the ironic Edith Agonistes, Wharton utilizes fiction as the weapon with which she simultaneously fights these moral fights, and embraces modern ambiguity (171). "The way to salvation and happiness, for Wharton, led through the much more

---

[3] This appears in a letter of May 25, 1937 -- Lilly Library (Bauer 165).

complex terrain of cultural contradictions, by embracing the ambivalence that was so much a part of modern life for her. To see the 'beyondness of things'… was the goal of her 'inner life'" (178).

Another significant contribution to the short story criticism is Carol Singley's *Edith Wharton: Matters of Mind and Spirit* which appeared on the Wharton criticism scene in 1995. Her book is a discussion of Wharton as a novelist of morals as well as manners, of spirit as well as society. Singley examines the religious and philosophical questions informing Wharton's work, placing it against the backdrop of turn-of-the-century scientific, philosophic, social and aesthetic debates. She argues compellingly that Wharton's religious and philosophical views are her personal response to a broader cultural crisis of belief, due in part to the waning power and importance of religion in people's day-to-day lives. Wharton's fiction demonstrates how she accepted, challenged and adapted both classical and Judeo-Christian traditions. In particular, Wharton responds in her fiction to the American literary traditions of Calvinism, Transcendentalism, modernism and realism. We have "looked for Edith Wharton in the drawing room," but we must also look for her "in the library, voraciously consuming volumes" in an intellectual and spiritual search for absolute values that she never found, and ideals from which she fell short (x-xii).

Singley's discussion covers a wide range of Wharton's fiction. She discusses *The House of Mirth* and the crisis of faith, *Ethan Frome* and the Calvinist tradition, and *The Reef* and *Summer* and American transcendentalism as represented by Emerson and Whitman; she then moves on to an analysis of *The Age of Innocence* and Platonic Idealism, and concludes by investigating Wharton's attraction to Catholicism and the two novels *Hudson River Bracketed* and *The Gods Arrive*. Interspersed throughout the book, and most extensively in her first chapter are brief discussions of many of Wharton's short stories, serving as examples of the spiritual and philosophical quest in which Wharton engaged.

Even more recently, Carol Singley's important essay "Edith Wharton's Ironic Realism" in *Challenging Boundaries: Gender and Periodization* (2000) explicitly names Wharton as an "ironic realist" in the way she portrays the everyday experiences of characters whose choices often conflict with what society deems acceptable (226): "Wharton is a subtle but forceful social and moral critic of the world she depicts. Irony is the means by which she both exposes her characters' foibles and deals debilitating blows to their value systems" (227). Putting Wharton's writing into the context of sentimental, realist and naturalist literature, Singley argues that Wharton's fiction, short and long, stems from but ultimately rejects the sentimental tradition from which she writes by virtue of her own womanhood, irony providing the "best vehicle for voicing concerns about woman's roles and opportunities" (229). Citing stories such as "The Other Two," "The Pelican," "The Angel at the Grave," Singley posits that the early fiction in general implicitly critiques sentimental fiction, showing the irony of how traditional women's roles limit or conflict with their intellectual lives (229, 233).

Comparing Wharton to naturalists such as the intellectual historian Hippolyte Tain and George Eliot, and realists such as William Dean Howells, Singley argues that Wharton's fiction differs not only from sentimental fiction, but also from that of the naturalists and realists – Tain's theories, for example, are morally neutral where in Wharton's fiction aesthetic value is always intertwined with moral value (237-238); Wharton isn't really a naturalist despite her deterministic bent; her characters strive to meet ideals, artistic and moral, and continually fall short. Similarly, where Howells places characters within social communities, Wharton emphasizes characters' isolation from those communities (232). Singley states that Wharton is a realist, but one who "push[es] against the boundaries of the period" (240).

Both Bauer and Singley make great strides in adding new depth to Wharton criticism, Bauer by discussing novels that are rarely considered, and

Singley in terms of the wide range of work that she discusses. Both writers also bring a whole new dimension to Wharton studies by making specific comparisons to culture and to the history of ideas, both intellectual and popular, that inform her writing. Furthermore, both of these writers see the importance of irony in understanding Wharton's stance and technique as an artist confronting the late nineteenth-century world of the sentimental. But the primary focus of both of these writers is, conventionally, on the novels. Bauer does allocate a whole chapter to "Roman Fever," but this story is the most well-known, the most frequently anthologized, and the most often discussed. Bauer therefore does not add much new knowledge to the understanding of Wharton's enormous short story canon as a whole. Singley does just the opposite – she covers an enormous number of short stories in both of her discussions, but the effect of this is to not give nearly enough detailed and sustained attention to the best of the stories.

There are, however, two excellent full-length studies entirely devoted to the short stories, Barbara A. White's *Edith Wharton: A Study of the Short Fiction* (1991), and Evelyn Fracasso's *in Edith Wharton's Prisoners of Consciousness* (1994). White's study is introductory, providing a general perspective of Wharton's short fiction and the characteristic themes and techniques. White examines Wharton's body of short fiction chronologically, focusing on Wharton's change in emphasis, rather than on her evolution as a short story writer. Her early works establish Wharton as an artist, who experiments with narrative point of view. The early stories have both male and female narrators and protagonists, and are not especially class-conscious (27). Her early stories share the themes of the responsibilities of the artist, the nature of art and perception, courage and cowardice, past and present, and female experience, including marriage, divorce, and a preoccupation with father-daughter incest (27, 50-59). In the early works, White finds no thematic attention to the economics of marriage, nor with either the supernatural or the decline of Old New York. The fiction written from 1902 to 1916 includes Wharton's best collections, White contends, *The Descent of Man* and *Xingu* (57). The stories from this middle period are thematically consistent with the earlier work, but with a different focus: Wharton examines the economic consequences of marriage and divorce, artistic consequences for economic benefits, and her incest themes focus on women's complicity in the situation (57). Unlike the earlier stories, White notes, Wharton's short fiction from this middle period primarily uses male narrators and focuses more on the upper class than on the middle or lower classes (57-58). White suggests that Wharton returns in her later work to female narrators and to many of her early themes in a manner less conservative but sharper, more unrelentingly biting, ironic and satirical towards her characters and their situations (xii, 84-88). She adds to her earlier themes the subjects of old age, illness, and death, and reexamines characters who are not members of the upper class. What makes Wharton less, and not more, conservative in the later short fiction, White argues, is Wharton's use of these themes and subjects to examine the dispossessed and the powerless, those on the fringes of society (88-89).

White's study is successful in planting Wharton's work squarely in the twentieth century, showing implicitly that Wharton's thematic concerns are modern concerns shared by other modern writers, and that the later short stories are no less worthy of critical attention than her earlier ones. Evelyn E. Fracasso, in *Edith Wharton's Prisoners of Consciousness* (1994), tacitly agrees that the later work is by no means weaker than the earlier, discussing the theme of imprisonment, and the techniques of portraying it in the short stories. Fracasso looks at imprisoned characters and the devices Wharton uses to convey their imprisonment by pairing early and later stories organized around four themes: love and marriage, society, art and morality, and fear of the supernatural (4-8). Essentially Fracasso argues that Wharton develops as a technician by employing many devices to emphasize her protagonists' imprisonment in the early tales: symbolic settings, enclosed spaces, nature images, and omniscient narrators (12,

39,70). In the later stories, Wharton's technique expands the imprisonment images, such as bolted doors, clanking chains, and hand and eye images (12); in the later tales Wharton also uses more irony and satire, time shifts such as the flashback, frame narratives, surprise endings, significant names and physiognomy to reinforce the portrayal of inner consciousness revealed by interior monologues (40). Often surprise endings and the lack of interior monologues, Fracasso indicates, are the sources of weakness in some of the earlier short stories (52).

Fracasso concludes that Wharton is a fine technician of the form, despite not being an innovator, and is therefore worthy of more laudatory critical attention. Both White and Fracasso make strides in removing the stigma of "anachronistic" or "Victorian" from the reputation of Edith Wharton, identifying modernist characteristics in her short stories such as the stream-of-consciousness interior monologue, and her concern with consciousness in general. Wharton herself decries the disorganization of stream-of-consciousness writing in James Joyce, but she is quite willing to utilize it in the short stories to further her thematic explorations. Though perhaps we would not yet want to make the claim that Wharton is really America's Virginia Woolf, thanks to these two studies we can avoid the inaccurate cliché of labeling her the American Jane Austen, out of time and out of touch.

While both White and Fracasso seriously evaluate Wharton's short fiction and are therefore laudable, neither critic truly deals in depth with the wide scope of theme in the short fiction: neither critic really demonstrates successfully the brilliance of Wharton's short stories. White's discussion provides a solid introduction to those unfamiliar with the stories, but again, in trying to cover as many of them as possible, she examines few of them in sufficient detail. And while Fracasso's book is the first to treat Wharton seriously as a fine technician in her craft, avoiding the conventional opinion that short fiction is a lesser art form than the novel, Fracasso's analysis at times reads like a catalogue of techniques rather than a discussion of the relative successes and failures of their implementation. Clearly, these authors have proven that the short fiction merits critical attention, and have provided other scholars with a strong foundation of ideas and analyses upon which to build further analyses.

Much of this attention has been from the camp of feminist criticism. But Wharton's female characters, whether or not they achieve self-realization, are not merely victims of a patriarchal society or of relationships with men. Such a view is not only limiting; it renders impotent some of the female characters who refuse to be victimized. Is Mrs. Amyot in "The Pelican" a victim, or a self-possessed, shrewd woman who carves a niche for herself in a male world? Is Lydia in "Souls Belated" a victim of Gannett's conventionality, or is she courageous in her forcing of the issue of marriage? Is conventionality itself always wrong, or weak, or cowardly? Wharton does not always condemn the status quo, and to read her work as doing so is to oversimplify what both Bauer and Singley correctly establish as a complex relationship between a writer and the culture about which, through which, and for which she writes. Wharton's characters are, male or female, subject to the processes by which we as humans participating in our culture encode and internalize cultural ideologies. Whether these characters are victimized by this culture and these processes remains to be seen. Much of the feminist criticism Wharton's short stories receive remains locked in what Annette Zilversmit calls "the house of feminist protest, where society is always male dominated and female suffering is mostly male inflicted" (326). As Zilversmit suggests, it is time to move Wharton out of the arena of "feminist protest" fiction, and to examine Wharton as a "psychological novelist"; clearly, much work is still to be done.

The above discussion does not take into account articles pertaining to individual short stories, of which there are a great many; the aim here is to provide an overview of the most in-depth of the number of works dealing with Wharton's short stories in general. There are an even smaller number of critical analyses that deal with Wharton and irony, leaving much room for further exploration. Of course, many other writers have commented on Wharton's pervasive ironic sensibility: Arthur Hobson Quinn, in his introduction to *An Edith Wharton Treasury*, calls "The Other Two" a "masterpiece of irony"; Blake Nevius says that Wharton focuses on specifically American ironies (intro. vi-vii). Elizabeth Ammons, in *Edith Wharton's Argument With America*, argues that Wharton reveals the inconsistencies and ironies of her society (19); Patricia Plante notes Wharton's preoccupation with "the irony of things" in "The Descent of Man" and in "The Hermit and the Wild Woman" (366); Grace Kellogg sees Wharton's ironic sensibility as the "thread through all," citing rhetorical irony as Wharton's "natural weapon" (235, 241). There are, however, five works that deal explicitly with the function of irony in Wharton's work; none deals solely with the short stories.

Judith P. Saunders' brief essay on *The Bunner Sisters* is the first to deal specifically with irony and Wharton. Saunders presents the novella as an anti-bildungsroman that details the ironic reversals in expectations that Ann Eliza undergoes through the course of the story: first, she acknowledges that her sister might be vain and selfish (241-242). Then she learns that the proposal she assumed would be for her sister would be for her, and that she cared more than she ever realized she would to have this knowledge. Both her expectations for her sister and for herself are reversed (242). Her expectations of Ramy and his suitability as a husband are destroyed when Evalina returns ill, abused and dying, thus overturning her expectations of Evalina's future as well (243). But most ironic of all is the outcome of what Ann Eliza thought was a deed of self-sacrifice: "Self-sacrifice may be the ultimate presumption. Ann Eliza fails miserably at living second-hand through her sister; the final bitter irony of her story is that she might just as well have lived for herself" (245).

Lawrence J. Dessner in "Edith Wharton and The Problem of Form" stays within the mainstream of general negative opinion of Wharton and of her short stories; he mentions the short stories in defining Wharton's ironic method: "retrospective irony" (57). Retrospective irony is the establishing implicitly on the first page what the outcome will actually be on the last (57). Wharton uses retrospective irony frequently in the short stories via twist or surprise endings: "the end illuminates the beginning, and exposes the ingenuity of the author" (57).

But Dessner faults Wharton for her ingenuity, claiming that often it is this and not "any virtue on the part of a well-developed character that lies at the heart of the typical Wharton story (57). Furthermore, Dessner finds that it is this ingenuity of retrospective irony that weakens her novels; for example, in *The House of Mirth*, by establishing all of the irony in the first several pages, Wharton thus "exhaust[s]" the form, turning it into an episodic or picaresque novel that misses an "overall design"(57). Retrospective irony is more successful in *Ethan Frome*, which replaces the "episodic formlessness" of *The House of Mirth* with a Jamesian reflector who holds the narrative together, thus allowing the retrospective irony to function successfully (58). But Dessner glibly mentions that *Ethan Frome* is really a long short story published as a novel, and therefore the success of the retrospective irony technique has not really been proved in a longer form (58).

Carol Miller also discusses irony in *The House of Mirth* in her essay "'Natural Magic,' Irony as Unifying Strategy in *The House of Mirth*" (1985), but unlike Dessner, who attributes the weaknesses in Wharton's novels to her use of irony, Miller finds it to be her strength and center of her artistic imagination (82). Irony unifies her novels by establishing bonds between author, audience and the text, thus creating readers who are sensitive to multiplicity of meaning, to ambiguity and become "co-creators of meaning" (83). Irony thus becomes the most useful technique by which Wharton can portray her "vision of alienation" (83).

Miller enumerates four ironic devices that Wharton uses consistently in her novels and short fiction: ironic characterizations of protagonists and other characters, ironic situations, patterns of recurring imagery that have a cumulative ironic effect, and most interestingly, the interplay in her fiction of elements of romance, realism and naturalism for ironic effect (83). *The House of Mirth*, though somewhat naturalistic or deterministic in its treatment of fate or chance, avoids determinism through Lily's personal evolution. Wharton is able to "transcend" a determinist vision because her "fictive perception arises primarily from an ironic, rather than a determinist perspective" (85). Thus we find many romantic elements in Wharton's work overall: the use of the "exotic" or supernatural, her lush natural descriptions, her "admiration for individuality and...preserving free will," and her "irrepressible fascination with beauty" (86). *In The House of Mirth*, Wharton "layers" ironic meaning: Lily has both romantic and physical "instincts" that challenge circumstance, blending naturalist and romantic elements for "ironic effect" (86).

Katherine Hadley Miller's essay dealing with irony in *The Age of Innocence* also contributes to the idea that irony is Wharton's artistic strength and not, as Dessner would suggest, her weakness. Wharton's "ironic undermining" of the novel's structure allows her to avoid a "traditional nineteenth century ending" (262). The novel is a bildungsroman in which Newland Archer is the American hero on a quest for self-definition (264). He searches for a new "land," thinking he might find it in Ellen's world, certain he will not find it in May's (264). But underneath is Ellen's bildungsroman: her journey to and from New York, and her changing perspectives on New York (266). Wharton ironically undermines Newland's story by "reminding us" of what Ellen does not say, or does not hear said, focusing on "Newland's obsessive curiosity about it – a curiosity that is fed by Ellen's own willingness to leave her story untold" (266). Newland's quest, ironically, becomes a search for information about Ellen (266). May's story is also untold; the irony is that Newland is utterly uninterested in May's story until after her death, when it is too late to ever hear it directly (267). Miller argues that Wharton heaps irony on the story even in the end, where rather than using the traditional death-or-marriage bildungsroman ending, the novel is open-ended, and Newland's motives for his choice seem also to be untold (270). And only Ellen has, of all of them, remained free (270).

What, artistically, was Wharton responding to when she chose irony as the main technique for exploring these themes? Perhaps she was reacting against the dryness of realism as much as she was reacting against the romantic sentimentalism into which the lofty, idealistic early nineteenth-century fiction had disintegrated. Much of the recent criticism of Wharton's work, as I have already discussed, has concerned itself with Wharton's conscious and unconscious connections to the culture surrounding her, intellectual, literary and popular alike, but only mentions the short stories tangentially

Thus, this study will attempt to uncover both the different levels of ironic effect in the short stories, and also the means by which Wharton achieves her complexity. My argument assumes Wharton's ironic philosophy and focuses on the formal aspects that are inextricably tied to expressing such a vision: irony as the formal reaction against the formal looseness and "sentimental undergrowth" of popular fiction (Wharton *A Backward Glance* 141). This reaction parallels a concept of the universe grounded in reason and therefore relativity – science and determinism – and reacts against the fogginess of romantic idealism and sentimentalism and its manifestations of a hazy view of the cosmos as inherently good and getting better. Realism and naturalism are alternative formal-philosophical responses that Wharton experiments with implicitly in her fiction, and ultimately rejects as unsatisfactory, the former because it portrays a world without human ideals, and the latter because the ideals it portrays are scientific, dehumanized and dehumanizing. Wharton's ultimate goal is clarity, even if ultimately clarity of a vision of ambiguity.

My understanding of Wharton's ironic technique centers around the relationship between Wharton as ironist, the narrative strategies she employs in conveying irony to the audience, and how the audience receives and reacts to her irony. Among these three poles lies the irony itself, which is in this context perhaps the more easily understandable aspect of Wharton's ironic technique. To understand this complex relationship, we must put aside current discussions of irony as a consciousness of one's belatedness or as a means of provoking readers into a state of uncertainty about the status of texts or of how their meanings are determined, or of our very cognitive ability to understand. Understanding Wharton's irony requires more specific and formal definitions of irony and how they function within the relationship of ironist-audience-narrator. Walter Ong, in his discussion of irony and mimetic theory, mentions the role and the use of the unreliable narrator that Wayne C. Booth, in *The Rhetoric of Fiction,* finds to be one of the main generators of ironic effect: "The obvious sense is not to be trusted" because the person producing the utterance is more and more distanced from the audience of that utterance – distance caused by writing and especially by print (27). To Ong and others, irony as a basic literary strategy, a distancing strategy by which writers create "multi-layers" of irony in service of creating a "'pure' literature in which the literary content would simply constitute its own world," is becoming less and less of a possibility in an electronic age of "secondary orality" (32). As Bauer suggests, Wharton sensed these technological changes and was creates a pure fictive world in touch with the mass culture to which she was reacting.

D.C. Muecke's categorizations of irony in *The Compass of Irony* also elucidate the nature of the relationship between ironist, audience and narrator or narrative strategy. Muecke sees irony as a "double-layered phenomenon": the lower level is the "victim's" perspective of a particular situation or the presentation of this perspective by the ironist (19). The upper level is the situation from the ironist's or observer's perspective (19). This upper level is not necessarily made explicit in the text (19). Irony is generated by the contradiction or incongruity between these two levels: what is said contradicts what is meant, or what the victim of irony thinks contradicts what observer knows (19).

Muecke then mentions two kinds of irony: simple irony, in which the incongruity is between the two levels, and double irony, in which the incongruity exists entirely within the lower level (20). Simple irony is the most familiar, incorporating verbal irony, or irony of language, as well as situational irony in which the discrepancy between "an ostensibly true statement, serious question, valid assumption, or legitimate expectation" is "corrected, invalidated, or frustrated by the ironist's real meaning, by the true state of affairs, or by what actually happens" (23). Double irony occurs when two equally invalid perspectives invalidate one another, or when the victim sees both contradictory terms as equally valid, resulting in paradoxes, dilemmas, or impossible situations (24-25). Double irony is the more "philosophical" and more modern kind of irony because it is not merely corrective; it is philosophical in the sense that such ironies deal with contradictions of human nature or the human condition, and it is more modern since it is more self-conscious, "more tentative (lacking the element of resolution) and more open to dialectic opposition" (26-27). Though Wharton almost reflexively employs simple ironies where and when useful, it is her employment of double irony that marks her as an ironist par excellence.

Muecke asserts that the traditional definitions of verbal and situational irony are limited; and within the context of defining verbal irony as conscious employment of a technique rather than the "situational" condition of affairs or outcome of events due to life, fate or chance, Wharton is clearly a verbal ironist, but this term is insufficient, especially given the strong determinist streak that runs throughout her work and particularly throughout the short stories (42-44).

Muecke identifies an irony of events. When an expectation is unmet, or when the opposite or negation of expectation occurs, the irony of events is the "confident unawareness" of any outcome other than the one expected (31-32). Wharton employs this kind of irony by using what Lawrence Dessner identifies as "retrospective irony" (or Booth's dramatic irony) presaging the outcome of the end of the narrative in the first paragraph, page, or chapter: but all are confidently unaware of the outcome, audience and ironic victim alike.

Muecke discusses levels or amounts of irony by distinguishing between grades of irony (the extent to which meaning is concealed, covert or overt) and modes of irony (the kind of relationship between irony and ironist: impersonal, self-disparaging, ingénue, dramatized) (53). In irony at the overt level, both the victim and the reader are meant to see the ironist's real meaning immediately; the contradiction is obvious and is often achieved by tone (54-55). Covert irony is less obvious, and tone would not immediately reveal it: the ironist uses "innocent" non-ironical language while simultaneously allowing the "real" meaning to be discovered (56). Private irony is irony intended for the ironist alone, either for personal amusement or as a means of releasing unpleasant or inappropriate feelings (59-60).

According to Muecke there are four modes of irony. First, impersonal irony provides us with the ironist him or herself as a persona, a voice of reason: a "mask" allowing the ironist to say what he or she means (61-62). Second, self-disparaging irony establishes a persona who expresses opinion in opposition to the 'real' opinion of the ironist (62). Ingénue irony gives us no persona; the ironist partially withdraws, speaking through another (62). Finally, in dramatized irony, the ironist entirely withdraws. Only the event narrated is itself ironic, and the audience must discover the irony alone (63); such irony "mirrors" ironies in life's real situations (63). Wharton's ironies operate mainly in the realm of the covert, not in the extremes of the overt or the private. But her use of different modes of irony creates degrees of overtness. Though not so easily fit into Muecke's classification of the modes, Wharton's ironic narrative strategies might nevertheless be categorized in terms of the ironist's involvement. Appropriating

June Howard's terms of the detached "observer" and the tangentially involved "spectator" from the world of the naturalistic to the world of the ironic is useful here: we can redefine Muecke's "impersonal persona" of the ironist as the observer, the disembodied voice of reason and reality who, as the third person omniscient narrator, interrupts the narrative to comment ironically on the action of the narrative, and on the characters and their various roles in that action. But to discuss Wharton, we must collapse the "self-disparagement" category with the ingénue category, since her reflector narrators are never obviously in opposition to her as ironist; nor are they clearly the mouthpieces through which she speaks: the relationship between Wharton and her reflectors is ambiguous and perhaps itself ironic. Better to call this category or mode that of the mediatory "spectator" who is marginally involved in the story objectively enough, or thinks him or herself so, to comment upon the other characters and their situation, and to draw his/her own conclusion. Finally, we enter Howard's "brute" category of the unaware but naturalistically determined individual, who in our ironic world becomes Muecke's dramatized irony: no omniscient narrator observes the action; no reflector character spectates. We are alone with the characters, and, in a suppression or withdrawal of narrator altogether, we are brutally forced into the minds of the ironized characters themselves, viewing the unfolding of events either from one subjective point of view or from shifting, multiple points of view.

Building on Muecke's discussion of "grades of irony," which define the extent to which meaning is concealed, Wayne C. Booth classifies ironies as overt or covert, stable or unstable, and either local, limited or infinite. Stable irony is Muecke's "rhetorical irony" (48). We find stable ironies in the author's tone, in titles, epigrams, prefaces, postscripts, or in "known error proclaimed" (53-62). We may also see stable ironies via stylistic clashes, shifts, and stylistic parodies (63-68).

Booth defines rhetorical irony as intentional, intended by one human being to be shared by another (234). He classifies irony according to its degree of openness or disguise as overt or covert, and according to their degree of stability in reconstruction: can we assume that once we reconstruct a covert irony or understand an overt one, that our understanding and our reconstructive task are complete (234)? He also classifies ironies according to the scope of the truth revealed: is it a local truth, a truth that is limited and thus finite, or is it "'absolute infinite negativity'" (234)?

Wharton does not often, if ever, employ stable overt ironies, whether local or infinite – she rarely simply asserts an ironic perspective. She does, however, utilize stable covert ironies, local, limited, and infinite. Booth elaborates that stable-covert-local irony as already defined has hidden meanings that, once discovered, are fixed, and will be read the same way by "qualified readers" regardless of subjective differences between them (235). Muecke points out that until well into the eighteenth century, this was how irony was defined (235).

The critic Gary Handwerk, however, takes issue with Wayne C. Booth's "normative" irony. While approving of and finding useful Booth's categories, he finds them unable to deal with more complex instances of irony because they are too static, and too "individualist," too contained in self-perceptions (6-8). Booth, Handwerk contends, fails to see the "dialectical power of irony" (8): drawing on Lacan, Handwerk sees what he calls "ethical" irony as an essentially communal process, a social act in which self-knowledge emerges and is dependent upon interaction with another subject (4-5). Booth ignores this idea of "intersubjectivity" (169-170).

What Muecke and Booth call unstable ironies are ironies in which no fixed reconstruction is possible (Booth 240). The author hides him or herself, not embracing a fixed truth; no clear affirmation is available except the affirmative rejection of affirmation in general, or, as Handwerk further suggests, only "situational truth[s], what will suffice here and now," and not absolutes, can exist

(Booth 240; Handwerk 16). Irony emerges through dialogue, through social intercourse, as the negation of determinate meanings (Handwerk 17). Wharton uses irony "to interrogate, not to establish metaphorical equivalencies" – only to ask the questions, not to find absolutes (16, 172). Thus unstable infinite irony teeters towards the absurd, in which nothing can really mean what it says, because everything is subject to irony (241). Muecke calls this the transition from specific to general irony (241). We also see Wharton using these kinds of ironies as well, though rarely overtly, and rarely veering towards the extreme of the infinite absurdity. Rather, we find in Wharton's work unstable-covert-local and finite ironies that have many alternative hidden meanings, none of which is a certainty (249). This, then, is at the heart of Wharton's genius: ironic but not pessimistic, the majority of her work stays within the bounds of the covert but finite, flirting with the infinite, with instability, an ironic middle ground that accounts for her sympathy towards her characters, and her frequent sense of hope implicit in the open-endedness of her short stories, and allows her to ask questions without finding, or even needing, the answers.

I shall not attempt to discuss all or even most of the short stories, but rather examine in depth a relatively small group of stories that both represent the span of Wharton's literary career and represent many crucial instances of Wharton's complex ironic genius, which, like the overall quality of the stories themselves, never wavers from the early to the late short fiction. The stories I shall include from early in Wharton's career, 1895-1904, are "The Lamp of Psyche," published in *Scribner's Magazine* in October, 1895, but uncollected until the 1968 Lewis collection; "The Muse's Tragedy," published in *Scribner's* in January of 1899 and collected in *The Greater Inclination* in 1899; "Souls Belated," also collected in *The Greater Inclination*; "The Angel at the Grave," originally published in February, 1901, in *Scribner's* and collected in *Crucial Instances* in 1901; and "The Line of Least Resistance," originally published in

Lippincott's in October, 1900, and uncollected until the 1968 Lewis collection. Also from the early part of Wharton's career are "The Reckoning," originally published in August, 1902, in *Harper's Magazine* and collected in *The Descent of Man, and Other Stories* in 1904; "The Other Two," first appearing in *Collier's* in February, 1904, and also collected in *The Descent of Man*; "The Descent of Man," originally appearing in *Scribner's* in March of 1904 and collected in *The Descent of Man*; "The Last Asset," appearing in *Scribner's* in August, 1904, and collected in *The Hermit and The Wild Woman.*

From the middle part of Wharton's career, 1904-1916, I have chosen "Xingu," published first in *Scribner's* in 1911, and then collected in *Xingu and Other Stories*; "Autres Temps . . ." which first appeared in July, 1911 in *The Century Magazine* under the title "Other Times, Other Manners," and was collected with this title in *Xingu and Other Stories* in 1916; and "The Long Run," published in February, 1912, in *Atlantic Monthly* and also collected in *Xingu and Other Stories.*

From the final phase of Wharton's career, 1916 until her death in 1937, I shall examine "The Temperate Zone," originally appearing in *Pictorial Review* in February, 1924, collected in 1926 in *Here and Beyond*; "Pomegranate Seed," published in April, 1931, in the *Saturday Evening Post* and collected in 1936 in *The World Over*; and "Confession," first appearing in *Hearst Magazine* in 1936, then included in *The World Over* also in 1936. All of the above-mentioned stories have also been collected in the 1968 Lewis edition of the short stories. In choosing these stories and omitting others, I have attempted to present a diverse number of stories from her early, middle and late work, while also choosing what I consider to be representative of Wharton at her creative best.

The rest of my study is organized into four chapters: Chapter One, "Irony and the Observer Narrator," will examine Wharton's more "conventional" ironic structure and use of a third-person omniscient observer narrator. When Wharton herself is the narrator she is similar to Jane Austen as narrator, as an old-fashioned omniscient narrator of manners commenting upon the characters whose story she narrates. Such ironies are, as Booth classifies them, stable and covert ironies that she and the audience form through the creation of an "ironic interaction" between the audience, herself, and the text. We are told by this observer-narrator, through the tone and flippant wit (among other things) with which she turns on her characters, that a particular character thinks of him or herself in one way, but fails to see the reality of his or her own situation, at least at first, if ever. These characters are moral idealists; irony, often a retrospective irony here as perhaps one of the most stable kinds of covert irony, is generated when they take part in their own realistic undermining. The narrator's role here is to make us aware that something unexpected is going to occur, through all sorts of local verbal commentaries. Stories in this category are "The Lamp of Psyche," "The Line of Least Resistance," "The Angel at the Grave," "The Descent of Man," and "The Reckoning."

In Chapter Two, "The Ironic Spectator," I will evaluate Wharton's use of a reflector or spectator narrator who watches the central action of the protagonists without necessarily participating in it. Such a character reflects upon or interprets the events before him or her, often, though not always, in first person, and offers his or her opinion to the audience, acting as the ironic pointer. It is the spectator whose commentary through which we, the audience, see, making us once removed from Wharton herself. Wharton is not merely speaking through these characters; who they are and what their roles are affect the delivery of their reflections. To an extent, the irony generated here rebounds on both the characters who are at the center of the action, and on the reflector him or herself; this character is often the idealist who thinks he or she sees "true reality" from the actions of the other characters, naive and innocent of irony though they may be. And as the ironic mode distances us from the ironist, the ironies themselves thus become less stable, less fixed. We have perhaps moved from the more stable to the less stable, from the local to the limited or finite. Stories in this category include "The Other Two," "The Last Asset," "The Long Run," and "The Temperate Zone."

In Chapter Three, "Self-Conscious, Self-Ironized," I analyze Wharton's use of interior monologue and other devices to counter "fictive reality" with the "psychological reality" of her characters and the ironic discrepancy between the two. The third narrative strategy producing irony is the suppression or absence of an observer or spectator-narrator and the forcing of an intimate relationship between the audience and the characters themselves. This kind of irony resembles Booth's category of "covert infinite" irony: a vision of continually undermined irony, for which there are few resolutions or fixities. The ultimate irony is of such an ironized character's mistakenly thinking him or herself at the height of idealistic success in completing his or her event. We see this through reflections revealed: no Whartonian ironist is visible at all. Irony thus emerges from the gap between our whole picture and the protagonist's one-sided view. Irony is generated by this and by the characters themselves either by the double irony of reaching a conscious understanding of the "real" situation but being unable to change or affect it in any way, or by never understanding that the discrepancy exists in the first place. In this category we find two kinds of protagonists: We find unconscious and therefore ironic characters in "Full Circle," and self-conscious, and therefore self-ironic characters appear in such stories as "The Muse's Tragedy," "Souls Belated," "Autres Temps . . ." and "Pomegranate Seed." It is with the interpretive open-endedness of this last group of stories that Wharton approaches instabilities that flirt with, if never fully achieve, the infinite. Chapter Four will be a concluding chapter, in which Wharton's ironic genius is made relevant through a discussion of the literary and cultural climate in which Wharton was writing and to which she was responding.

Chapter One
Irony and The Observer Narrator

"The Lamp of Psyche" reflects the "'full play,'" as Cynthia Griffin Wolff calls it, of irony in the early short stories through the use of an omniscient narrator. Published in *Scribner's Magazine* in October of 1895, this story demonstrates both Wharton's ironic technique and what M.M. Brown calls Wharton's "ironic philosophy." In this story, as in many of Wharton's early stories, marriage is the thematic instrument upon which Wharton's editorial observer plays. Delia Corbett's ideals, this observer points out, become her own undoing. Wharton employs two techniques to achieve this: first, through her narrator's editorial comments, which provide an ironic stance through which she manipulates her audience into alliance. Second, Wharton employs ironies via offhand comments made by characters that are loaded with significance, but a significance that only reveals itself to readers retrospectively.

The very opening of the story introduces us to this editorial observer, who looks down on Delia and her husband from some superior place. And in the very opening, Wharton foreshadows with this ironic voice a discrepancy between what Delia believes to be her reality at this point, and what she will truly see as real by the end of the story: "her happiness almost touched the confines of pain – it bordered on that sharp ecstasy which she had known, through one sleepless night after another when what had now become a reality had haunted her as an unattainable longing" (Wharton, "The Lamp of Psyche" 42). Immediately Wharton establishes an ironic interaction between the observer, us, and the text. Such extreme, even painful happiness, as the fulfillment of Delia's "unattainable longing," is immediately suspicious as soon as the observer presents it as Delia's reality. The narrative voice continues to dissect Delia, dripping with sarcasm. Prior to her marriage to Corbett, Delia "took herself, as a rule, rather flippantly, with a dash of contemptuous pity," but now "it became her to pay herself an almost reverential regard" because "Love had set his golden crown upon her forehead, and the awe of the office allotted her subdued her doubting heart" (42). Wharton hyperbolizes Delia's sense of importance and accomplishment at marrying Laurence Corbett; to all but her this is an "immense unapproachable privilege" (42). Here too, the observer's exaggerated tone and choice of words reveals the verbal irony that marrying Corbett, for whatever reasons, is not the "privilege" Delia thinks it to be. As Barbara White suggests, in this and other short stories, one of the themes to be considered is that of "male corruption, buried secrets, past-crimes unearthed" (49). That Wharton creates this gap between Delia's feelings about and understanding of Corbett, and that of the observer, who becomes our ally in understanding, suggests early on in the tale that something Delia does not yet know about her husband will be revealed. There exists an overt and a covert Corbett whom we discover through the aid of the observer.

Overtly, Corbett has an aesthetic eye: "The room in which she sat was very beautiful; it pleased Corbett to make all his surroundings beautiful" (Wharton 43). This, perhaps, is the key to our understanding of Corbett's earlier behaviors and to Delia's misreading of him and of them: if the world is a beautiful place, it is an easeful one, lovely, not difficult or challenging or confrontational. All must be, like Corbett's dinner parties, "delightful," not complicated or upsetting. And what delights Delia early in the story, symbolically imprisons her, as Fracasso points out (12); the small "ivy-walled garden," the "mellow bindings," the "deep-piled rugs, the pictures, bronzed, and tapestries," and all of the rarefied "conferences on art or literature" give her an "almost reverential regard" for Corbett himself (Wharton 43, 53, 42). And this regard, signified in all of Corbett's lovely belongings, entraps her in a set of illusions about Corbett and about herself, that, when undone, doubly entrap her in a marriage to a man that she ultimately cannot either admire or respect. Delia remembers the wonderful times spent at Corbett's while married to her first husband, desiring Corbett as her second. Wharton sets off warning signals early on with an editorial intrusion directed straight at the reader:

> The high-minded reader may infer from this that I am presenting him in the person of Delia Corbett, with a heroine whom he would not like his wife to meet; but how many of us could face each other in the calm consciousness of moral rectitude if our innermost desire were not hidden under a covenient garb of lawful observance? (43)

That is, the narrator partly excuses Delia's exuberant self-congratulation at attaining her innermost desire since she has attained it through the "lawful" means of marriage. Delia's "moral rectitude" very much rests in the fact that, though desiring Corbett while still married to Benson, she does not act on this desire until legally able to do so; no extramarital affairs for her! Wharton demonstrates the sharp, cold wit that so many critics find distasteful and unsympathetic in this "male readers' wives, beware" comment, but in the very same passage she reveals a sympathy for Delia's approaching predicament that many critics do not give her credit for; by addressing the reader directly, and by conspiratorily complimenting the reader as "high minded," Wharton's narrator becomes our ally, manipulating our vision of Delia into a sympathetic one even before we understand why we need to feel sympathetic towards her. Thus, we understand, initially, why Delia feels herself in the moral right. Delia's first husband, Benson, is a man of "indiscretions," as Wharton delicately says, a man of no scruples, and "no one," including us,

> would have blamed her if, with the acquirement of a fuller discrimination, she had thrown them [sentimental knick-knacks] all out of the window and replaced them by some object of permanent merit, but she was expected not only to keep Benson for life, but to conceal the fact that her taste had long since discarded him. (44)

Delia is, to this extent, the object of sympathy, married too young to an unfaithful and unscrupulous man, not only not able to end the marriage but unable even to express her dismay at her mistake except with a resigned sigh (44). Clearly, Delia was trapped; the only release from this imprisoning marriage was the near-miraculous event of Benson's death.

However, what compromises our sympathy for Delia is her willingness to become imprisoned once again. She married Benson "for love," love's ideal being for her at that point the "beautiful blue eyes" and charming, dandified "gardenia'd" appearance of her intended (44). In this passage, the observer is entirely un-ironic. Delia's sentimental girlhood visions of love and Benson were overturned by the reality of his despicable behavior, "smudg[ing] the whiteness of her early illusions" (44). But then our observer turns ironic once again: "It could hardly be expected that a woman who reasoned so dispassionately about her mistakes should attempt to deceive herself about her preferences" (44). It could hardly be expected that she would, and yet, we learn later in he story, she does: "Corbett personified all those finer amenities of mind and manners which may convert the mere act of being into a beneficent career; to Delia he seemed the most admirable man she had ever met, and she would have thought it disloyal to her best aspirations not to admire him" (44). But Delia has replaced one illusion with a far more insidious one: that the veneer of good looks and nice dress can be replaced with a veneer of "finer amenities of mind and manners"; the polished exterior is matched by a polished aesthetic interior. Corbett need not be anything other than ornamental – he need only look and sound good, and not necessarily do good to fulfill Delia's "best aspirations." Thus it is not only her ideal of Corbett that is shattered during their visit to America and Aunt Mary's, but more importantly, it is her ideal of herself, her powers of judgment and discernment, and her illusions about what her aspirations should be, that are shattered. The lamp that illuminates her misreading of Corbett illuminates her own self-misunderstanding. What implicates her even further is the superficiality of her own self-questioning:

> She asked herself perversely (she was given to such obliqueness of self-scrutiny) if to a dispassionate eye he would appear as complete, as supremely well-equipped as she beheld him, or if she walked in a cloud of delusion, dense as the god-concealing mist of Homer. But whenever she put this question to herself, Corbett's appearance instantly relegated it to the limbo of solved enigmas; he was so obviously admirable that she wondered that people didn't stop her in the street to attest to her good fortune. (45)

Again Wharton hyperbolizes, forcing us to see the extremity of Delia's self-delusions, and the paucity of her expectations. And yet these were expectations that had "haunted her as an unattainable reality" (45). Corbett, who is "so perilously like the phantasms of joy which had mocked her dissatisfied past," creates in her "an impulse to seize him and assure herself" that he is real and that he is hers (45). But her self-questioning is only momentary, and she resists the urge, while yet "mocked" by the phantasms of her delusion: this, and Corbett, is exactly what or whom she wanted.

Wharton's narrator is not the only one generating irony; her irony is even more covert when it is voiced by one of her characters, but it is only understandable retrospectively. Thus in the ensuing dialogue between herself and Corbett, who interrupts her reverie, it is he who voices the irony for the audience.

> "What -- all alone?" he said, smiling back her welcome.
> "No, I wasn't -- I was with you!" she exclaimed; then fearing to appear fatuous, added, with a slight shrug, "Don't be alarmed -- it won't last."
> "That's what frightens me," he added gravely. (45)

Delia laughs off his comment as a good joke, and reads the letter that will carry them to America. Corbett knows and has accepted who he is, and he appears at least superficially to understand that she has not. Wharton foreshadows here our retrospective understanding that the irony rests, not merely on Delia's unveiling of Corbett's "secret," which to him is no secret at all, but on Delia's recognition that ultimately her feeling "won't last" because her phantoms have not been assuaged. And, as she later comments about her Aunt Mary's injury, which is the reason for her visit, "'She'll think the universe has come to a standstill,'" to which Corbett responds, "'She'll find it hasn't'" (47). She replies, "'Ah, but such discoveries hurt – especially if one makes them late in life'" (47). Here again, this comment is doubly ironic because Delia herself unwittingly voices it. Wharton plays ironies off of one another, forcing the audience to ally itself with the ironic stance of the observer, and reinforcing the "correctness" of this stance (with respect to correctly interpreting and thus discovering the covert meanings) by doubling the less covert narratorial ironic stance with more retrospective ironies whose meanings only become clear to us after completion of the story.

The interplay between the observer's ironic voice and the unassuming but retrospectively ironic comments and actions of the characters themselves continues throughout the second and third "Aunt Mary" sections of the story. It is in the second section of the story that Wharton provides the antithesis of Corbett's delightful aestheticism; Aunt Mary Mason Hayne is "the chief formative influence" of Delia's childhood, the reformer figure so popular in American literature of the mid- to late nineteenth century. Delia's self-scrutiny originates from this influence. "Her parents had been incurably frivolous, Mrs. Hayne was incurably serious, and Delia, by some unconscious powers of selection, tended to frivolity of conduct, corrected by seriousness of thought" (48). Delia measures her life by Aunt Mary's "utilitarian standards," while not feeling the need to live up to them: "it lent relief to her enjoyment of the purposeless" (48). Wharton comes close to caricature in the following description of Aunt Mary and her home as a place in which "one saw at a glance that Mrs. Hayne had never had time to think of her house or her dress" (49). Both the woman and the house are slightly archaic: the artwork on the walls, the old-fashioned marble-topped tables, the outdated coal in the fireplace, even Mrs. Hayne's ancient gown, reveal the lack of concern for beauty and fashion of the woman who owns them. Aunt Mary's outmoded belongings are "redeemed from monotony" by "their freight of books," "the buff walls stenciled with a Greek border," creating an atmosphere suited for serious ideas and useful actions (49). It is here that Delia's young mind, formed by the frivolity of her parents, is polished, and it is this setting that puts Delia's dilemma in relief. Having spent some weeks with her Aunt and with Corbett, Delia and her aunt have a confidential chat about him in section three of the story; the verdict – "My dear, he's delightful" – provides Delia with the very words she longs to hear, because they echo her own feelings (51). But Aunt Mary probes more deeply into Corbett's past: why has he left America to live in Europe? How old is he? Was he in the war? And the answer to this question, that Delia does not think so, is deeply disturbing to her. "What else could he have been doing? But the very word, as she repeated it, struck her as incongruous; Corbett was a man who never did anything. His elaborate intellectual processes bore no flower of result; he simply *was* – but had she not hitherto found that sufficient?" (53). Not only is the idea of Corbett's lack of participation in the war and his potential cowardice what is upsetting to Delia, though indeed every man of the right age fought in the Civil War, and those who had not "she had never heard designated by any name but one" (52). More deeply disturbing to Delia is that she had never asked him why he had not fought, nor felt the need to; she had found him sufficient as he was.

In the final section of the story, Delia must confront Corbett with her question. Prior to their departure, however, Wharton provides us with another "crucial instance" of ironic interplay between what we, allied with the ironic narrator, observe, and the offhand comments made by the characters. But now Wharton effects a change:

> But Delia was firm; she did not wish to remain in Boston . . .
>   "You turncoat!" Corbett said, laughing. "Two months ago you reserved that sacred designation [home] for Boston."
>   "One can't tell where it is until one tries," she answered, vaguely...

> "Very well. But pray take note of the fact that I'm very
> sorry to leave. Under your Aunt Mary's tutelage I'm becoming a
> passionate patriot." (53)

The change is Delia's own dawning understanding of the man she has married and why she married him. "The recollection of her husband's delightful house in Paris, so framed for a noble leisure, seemed to mock the aesthetic barrenness of Mrs. Hayne's environment," and thus she hastened to leave (53). But here Wharton creates irony out of inversion. Obsessed with the question of Corbett's non-participation in the war, Delia naturally wishes to escape the person and the setting that precipitated it, and return to the setting that justified her choice of the man with whom she is returning. That she has changed, Corbett senses, but he attributes it to a case of "Paris fever." At this point in the story, Wharton moves from an editorial omniscient observer to a limited omniscient narrator: we hear the question "Why wasn't he in the war" reverberating through Delia's mind incessantly. "It rose up and lay down with her, it watched with her through sleepless nights, and followed her into the street; it mocked her from the eyes of strangers, and she dreaded lest her husband should read it in her own" (54). But until their return to Paris, she does not confront him; she rationalizes that "she had become overstrung in the high air of Mrs. Hayne's moral enthusiasms; all she needed was to descend again to regions of more temperate virtue" (54). Here again Wharton switches back to the voice of the editorial observer intruding into the stream of Delia's thoughts, and then a quick switch back to limited omniscient narration, revealing to us Delia's ability to maintain her ideal of Corbett long after it has actually been shattered:

> Then came a flash of resistance – the heart's instinct of self-
> preservation. After all, what did she herself know of her husband's
> reasons for not being in the war? What right had she to set down
> to cowardice a course which might have been enforced by
> necessity, or dictated by unimpeachable motives? Why should she
> not put to him the question which she was perpetually asking

> herself? And not having done so, how dared she condemn him
> unheard? (55)

Delia's initial state of self-righteousness is now shadowed by self-doubt; she justifies to herself her husband's seemingly amoral escape from the war, while condemning herself for even thinking of criticizing him. That she remains caught in the web of this internal dilemma for "a month or more," while continuing their "delightful" life of entertainment and artistic pleasure, reminds us that this is a web of her own spinning. To end her turmoil, all she need do is ask her question, yet she delays and delays.

Only the unexpected gift of a Civil War Cavalry officer's miniature can bring Delia to a questioning of Corbett's actions to Corbett himself. Wharton employs a less covert "situational irony" of coincidence and convenience that is not merely clever, but that underscores Delia's torment and her own cowardice in not being able to confront Corbett honestly from the time that the question first arose. Here too, Wharton's ironies accumulate and rebound upon one another, as a seemingly innocuous exchange retrospectively echoes with ironic significance: "'It was kind of you, Laurence, to buy this – it was like you.' 'Thanks for the latter clause,' he returned, smiling" (56). How much insight into her Corbett himself actually has is difficult to determine, yet his remark uncannily suggests that he is at least momentarily aware that she is not speaking merely of his thoughtfulness in putting the miniature "again into the possession of fellow countrymen" (56). Delia hedges the question, excusing his non-participation in the war for him as youthful illness or possible expatriation, until there is nothing left to ask but that single question at last: "'Then why weren't you in the war?' 'Really,' he responds, 'I don't think I know …and the truth is that I've completely forgotten the excellent reasons that I doubtless had at the time for remaining at home'" (56). She finally confronts him with the moral dilemma so torturous to her. "Reasons for remaining at home? But there were none; every man of your age went to the war; no one stayed at home who wasn't lame, or blind, or deaf, or ill, or – '" (56). Delia breaks off here; only prodding from Corbett forces her to say the word she had been thinking for months. "'Or—?' he said. 'Or a coward,' she flashed out. The miniature dropped from her hands, falling loudly on the polished floor . . . Its protective crystal had been broken by the fall (57).

That the shattered crystal represents her shattered ideals and illusions is perhaps Wharton's irony at its most overt; the observer narrator tells us so in elegant, yet sharp language, relating how much cheaper and authentic looking is the "piece of clear glass" that replaces the crystal. "And for the passionate worship which she had paid her husband she substituted a tolerant affection which possessed precisely the same advantages" (57). Ending where we began, with the ironic voice of the observer narrator, the more overt lesson Delia learns is apparent: her idealistic love for Corbett cannot hold up under moral scrutiny of the man himself, as he is and with all that he has not done, once she dons her glasses. "Corbett was perfectly charming" in later accepting her apology for "behav[ing] like a fool," and "it was inevitable that he should go on being charming until the end of the chapter. It was equally inevitable that she should go on being in love with him; but her love had undergone a modification which the years were not to efface" (57).

But this story is not merely a story of self-sacrifice or one of resignation, as Dale B. Flynn suggests (157). It is also a story of self-knowledge: Delia becomes aware of her lack of discrimination; she sees that her moral ideals float on nothing but her inherited sensibility and not on the application of it to her own life: "'I've told you...' Corbett says to her, 'that I was neither lame, deaf, blind nor ill. Your classification is so simple that it will be easy for you to draw your own conclusion'" (57). This is what Delia begins to recognize and also recognizes that Corbett has seen this before she herself has: her own simplicity, superficiality of thought, belief, and moral code that forms her judgments of others' actions, and not her own. The "milestone" she "passes in her existence" is that Psyche's lamp illuminates both of them, shedding light on what are to her poor choices, not once but twice, of a husband; because of her own moral vacuousness, she has chosen a husband who is also morally vacuous, if not entirely amoral: "For that long-past action was still a part of his actual being; he had not outlived or disowned it; he had not even seen that it needed defending" (57). It is only she who has not discerned this. Thus Delia not only sees her husband for who he really is, but sees herself reflected in him; ironically, our observer covertly points out, she has chosen aptly indeed.

Is the story flawed? Evelyn Fracasso concludes that Delia's transformation occurs too quickly, that she slips into resignation towards her marriage without the inner questioning we see prior to the confrontation, and that Wharton's use of only one flashback does not give Delia the sufficient depth of character that frequent time shifts do in later stories such as "The Letters" (Fracasso 16). But Delia's self-understanding and her coming to terms with Corbett's past take weeks, or even months. And after all, the very lesson Wharton's observer narrator wants us to learn is that Delia herself is morally bereft, superficial, and shallow. To criticize Wharton for not including more stream-of-consciousness at the end would be missing Wharton's point: that the change that began weeks ago for Delia, sensed by Corbett, was not realized by her, literally until the moment that the crystal shattered.

Wharton rather liked her uncollected story "The Line of Least Resistance," calling it her "'finest story to date'" (qtd. in Fracasso 21-24). But with the "friendly but critical" reaction of friend and mentor Henry James, Wharton never included this story in any of her collections (*Letters* 41-42). Conventionally, critics have followed James' lead, finding it to be one of her lesser stories, because it becomes melodramatic by its end (Flynn 71). However this tale, like "The Lamp of Psyche," reveals Wharton's masterful use of covert-stable irony through the use of the observer narrator, who points out the difference between the protagonist's idealized view of his life and its reality. The protagonist in this story wrestles with his individuality as he tries desperately to be both himself and a conformer to social conventions and mores, creating a discrepancy between what is and what appears to be (Brown 54-57).

This story is also divided into numbered sections. In the first section, Wharton's observer narrator, using a combination of hyperbole and understatement, ironically creates a picture of Mindon's world as he would like to see it. This story, like "The Lamp of Psyche," is introduced by the observer, whose editorial comments reveal a scorn for Mindon and his perception of himself. The narrator comments parenthetically that Mindon acts on "negative information" which is "the kind from which his knowledge of his wife's movements was mainly drawn" (Wharton 215). From the very beginning, Wharton creates a discrepancy between Mindon's view of himself and ours; again, we are allied with the observer narrator, who purposely distances us from Mindon at the very outset. Mindon, therefore, is not an object of pity or sympathy. The observer mocks Mindon's rationalization for Millicent's desultory behavior:

> As Millicent pointed out, she couldn't feed her friends on mutton chops and Vichy because of his digestive difficulty, nor could she return their hospitality by asking them to play croquet with the children because that happened to be Mr. Mindon's chosen pastime. If that was the kind of life he wanted to lead he should have married a dyspeptic governess, not a young confiding girl, who little dreamed what a marriage meant when she passed from her father's roof into the clutches of a tyrant with imperfect gastric secretions." (215)

That Millicent is selfish, unsympathetic with, and inconsiderate of the man she has married is apparent, but Mindon allows her full reign, even when admitting that "it did seem unjust" to him "that their life should be one long adaptation to Millicent's faults at the expense of his own" (215). He sees himself as "reap[ing] the advantages of his wife's domesticity" (215). Her faults, in fact, are not blameworthy but actually "the making of her," and she is "the making of him"

(216). Because of Millicent he has a grand home and social prominence, rather than being relegated to the "depressing promiscuity of hotel piazzas" (216). These, and not a loving, mutually respectful marriage, are what Mindon values; the maintenance of his ostentatious status quo, regardless of his personal inconveniences, is Mindon's main object, even though he indulges in brief spurts of annoyance. He sees the world through Millicent's eyes, in economic terms. Millicent is the "goose" who lays the golden eggs; he is the counter of the eggs, the accountant who tabulates the wealth that Millicent squeezes out of him. Even his paltry luncheon is carefully figured into the overall budget of his life – his "annual food consumption probably amounted to about half of one percent on his cook's perquisites, and of the other luxuries of his complicated establishment he enjoyed considerably less than this fraction" (215). Mindon measures everything in terms of its material value, even time. Thus his wife's unpunctuality aggravates him only slightly less than that of his daughters. Time is money, and Mindon hates to waste it.

His daughters, early trained by their mother, are equally as bad. They "already showed signs of finding fault" with everything as their mother does, "with as much ease and discrimination" (216). They have inherited Millicent's unpunctuality too, her carelessness and her selfishness. Here Wharton shows the true range of her mind, discussing Mindon's reaction to his family's indifference to him as a biological "Theory"; as the narrator reveals Mindon's theory that Millicent has "transmit[ted] an acquired characteristic to her children," passing on her "traits" to her "offspring," the narrator generates a double irony: first, that Mindon would rationalize away that which, at the very least, irritates him, and second, that he would turn, as so many literary figures of the period do, to a popularized version of heredity theory. Science, during this period, has reached the masses and Wharton, through her narrator's relaying of Mindon's typical rationalizations of his wife's behavior, seizes upon this pop science, ironically to explain what is clearly a socially learned behavior. Mindon considers the feeling of anger at his wife's and children's indifference to him to be "unreasonable," and "Mr. Mindon, who prided himself on being a reasonable man, usually found some other outlet for his wrath" (216). Mindon intentionally rationalizes away and thus misreads his true situation; he cannot or will not explain it for what it really is: his family's utter lack of consideration for him, a carelessness that excludes, and thus alienates him from the people to whom he should be the closest.

The irony of Mindon's self-delusion is magnified by a seemingly innocent conversation with his daughters about Gwendolyn's puppy, a gift from Millicent's lover Frank Antrim. When Mindon learns that Gwendolyn has been given a puppy, Mindon questions the gift and its giver:

> "Fwank Antwim," said Gwendolyn through a mouthful of mushroom soufflé.
> "Mr. Antrim," the governess suggested, in a tone that confessed the futility of the correction.
> "We don't call him Mr. Antrim, we call him Frank; he likes us to," said Gladys icily.
> "You'll do no such thing!" her father snapped. (217)

Why should Mindon mind a friendly gift, if that is all it was? He knows that Antrim is more than his wife's friend and daughters' gift-giver; Wharton underscores the significance of Antrim's role in Millicent's life by the insistent repetition of his name and Mindon's deliberate misunderstanding of it. Wharton cunningly substitutes the words "her father" for Mindon, reminding us of his role in the family, which is constantly being usurped. His daughters ally themselves with their mother and her lover: "We call him Frank; he likes us to," Gladys innocently remarks. Gladys' innocence contrasts sharply with the adulterous pair. Wharton creates a tension between the less covert narratorial ironies and this very covert retrospective one, whose meaning only becomes ironic once we actually understand that Millicent and Antrim are indeed having an affair. But doubly ironic is Mindon's ignorance, which is similar to Gladys' innocence insofar as both entail a lack of knowledge, but Mindon's seemingly innocent ignorance is compromised by the fact that he is a grown man, and not only should not be, but is not an innocent in every other aspect of the "business" that is his life. His response to his daughter's refusal to relinquish the puppy is to promise her "a much handsomer and more expensive one; his daughter should have a prize dog" immediately (217). Mindon is not naive, and should not be about his wife. It is not mere naivete but deliberate "schooling," training himself to be like Antrim out of a "high sense of propriety"; preserving his propriety is Mindon's defense for deliberately allowing himself not to see what he does not want to see.

Physical spaces in Wharton, as Evelyn Fracasso has demonstrated, often reflect a character's state of mind (71). Mindon's house and grounds reflect his economic values. His lawn looks "as expensive as a velvet carpet woven in one place," his garden only contains "expensive exotics," and Mindon revels in "the keen edge of" the "costliness" of the "scene" (Wharton 217). And yet he cannot take pleasure in the expensive things themselves, only in their expense: the marble statuary on his terrace does not seem to be "worth the price," and the fruit and flowers in his greenhouse, "the finest in Newport," "yielded at best an indirect satisfaction" since "he neither ate fruit nor wore orchids" (218). Mindon's sensibility is the polar opposite of that of Laurence Corbett: Corbett is the ultimate aesthete, valuing only art and beauty for its own sake. Usefulness – whether of art, or of Corbett himself – is not under consideration; he is utterly amoral. Mindon, however, values economic worth itself, lacking any appreciation for the intrinsic beauty of the things that he has acquired; their expense both impresses and worries him. "Mr. Mindon felt a natural pride in liking being rich enough to permit himself a perfectly useless room," but his study table, piled with bills, the dining and ball rooms, echoing past and future expensive dinners and dances, and his library, never read in, do not offer him the means for venting his displaced anger towards Frank Antrim (219). Even wandering into his daughters' room to play with them offers no respite for his turmoil, because they were dressing for a party and "took no notice of him" (218). This inattention echoes Gwendolyn's earlier comment that she does not "mind vexing papa -- nothing happens" (217). Mindon is their financial fount, but no more; neither can he gain his family's attention nor can he act on their behalf in any other way. He, like his library, is useless.

The "outlet" which Mindon seeks can only be found in his wife's boudoir, a useful room of "manifold purposes" (219). Mindon is "proud" of Millicent's "complex social system," which finds its headquarters in this room (219); he likes to "read over her daily list of engagements and the record of invitations she received in a season" even though he participates little in the activities of which she is at the center (219). Here too he sees things in economic terms; he is the outsider, the "modest investor," entering "the inner precincts of finance," and Millicent's social achievements are "perpetually swelling, like a rising stock" from which she might declare "an extra dividend" (219). Mindon's own descriptions of the physical spaces surrounding his daily life, seen through a moment of limited narration, reveal the depth of his rationalization of his family's treatment of him. If he can see things in financial terms, which he can understand, he does not have to confront and cope with what he cannot understand: his family's lack of regard or respect for him, and his wife's adultery. Only the coincidence of the revealing letter lying on the floor, combined with his "being a man of neat habits," forces him to face the reality of Millicent's affair (219). The story turns on this coincidence, but it is Mindon's very character traits that betray him: he is a man of reason, and thus able to reason away Millicent's unpunctuality; he is a man of propriety, and thus able to school himself into liking (or at least tolerating) his rival; he is a man of neat habits, and thus sets himself up to be the cuckold, the fool, when the letter shows him the truth. The irony here is generated not by hyperbole, as we saw previously, but more effectively by understatement. Wharton has no need to tell the audience what Mindon inadvertently reads; we know precisely what her ellipsis points represent. That the contents of the letter remain unspoken and unvoiced in Mindon's mind by a limited omniscient narrator emphasizes the depth of Mindon's previous denial of circumstances as they are and the profound turmoil into which his mind is thrown by this revelation.

The second part of the story retains both the observer narrator and the limited omniscient narrator; the limited omniscient narrator in this section reflects upon the disturbed contents of Mindon's mind, a new technique of Wharton's at this point in her career (Fracasso 21). Mere moments pass, but Mindon, possessed by an unimaginable rage, does not notice. But even now unable to direct his anger towards the person who deserves it, Mindon projects his anger onto the house, personifying it: "the room looked back at him, coldly, unfamiliarly, as he had seen Millicent look when he asked her to be reasonable. And who are you, the walls seemed to say" (219). Only through the metaphor of the house personified is Mindon able to express the rage he really feels towards Millicent in a rare moment of self-assertion:

> Why, if it weren't for me and my money you'd be nothing but a brick-and-plaster shell, naked as the day you were built -- no better than a garret or a coal hole. Why, you wouldn't *be* at all if I chose to tear you down. I could tear the whole house down, if I chose. (220)

D. B. Flynn points out that the rage he expresses here towards Millicent and her infidelity is an "ironic inversion of his earlier progress through the house" (Flynn 73). Also ironic is the time-conscious Mindon losing track of time. He was always consciously aware of time prior to finding the letter, but he is now "suddenly aware" of it, realizing that just moments before, he was not (220). "The clock struck and Mr. Mindon stood still," and he feels "omniscient," continuing to assert himself as he looks at his wife's picture, realizing that "for years he had been the man that Millicent thought him, the mere projection of her disdain; and now he was himself" (220). In an almost manic state, Mindon comes face to face with the rationalizing processes of his mind prior to finding the letter:

> His sudden translation to the absolute gave him a curious sense of
> spectatorship; he seemed to be looking on at his own thoughts. . .
> All the machinery worked with the greatest rapidity and precision
> . . .But suddenly he felt himself caught in the wheels of his terrific
> logic, and swept round, red and shrieking, till he was flung off into
> space. (220)

With the opening of the third part of the story comes the return of the observer narrator, and the return of Mindon's old habits of mind, "the old grooves," and instead of feeling alarmed by the ease with which his thoughts become self-justifications, Mindon instead feels "reassurance," and our observer narrator indicates the irony of this, scoffing that "his late ascent to the rarified heights of the unexpected had left him weak and exhausted" (221). Mindon's sense of propriety takes over as he congratulates himself that he has on "the right clothes," and has done "the proper thing" in leaving (221). "He was feeling, he was sure, as a gentleman ought to feel," calling up all of the "consecrated phrases" that express not his outrage but rather the proper and appropriate feelings: "outraged honor," "a father's heart," "the sanctity of the home" (221). But Mindon is unable to sustain an honest feeling or to express it for very long; rather, he worries over trivialities: "It was annoying not to get his letters. What would be done about them? Would they be sent after him? Sent where?" (221). He does not know where to go next, but worries more about the "propriety" of where to go, not why he should – even as he does (222). Ever aware of the passing of time, he realizes just how little his disappearance will figure into his family's life; Antrim can "fill his place" at Mrs. Targe's for dinner, and the girls "cherished him chiefly as a pretext, a sanctuary from bedtime and lessons. He had never in his life been more than an alternative to anyone" (222).

Uncomfortable from his "late adventure into the unknown," that the hotel to which he has removed himself represents, he is quick to revert to rationalization: "He had never before realized how much he loved his home"

(222). Mindon would rather be an alternative in someone else's life than be on his own, and he typically requires someone else's approval of his self-assertive action in order to "remain inflexible" (223). He gets the audience he desires in the form of three visitors, but in the fourth section of the story, he allows this audience and his sense of propriety to talk him back into the house and existence he had so recently renounced. He responds to the plea that he should consider his children with a justified "they've never considered me" (226). But his guests primly remind him that, according to society, it is he, and not Millicent, who "created the situation" "by making it known" (226). Mindon explains away his ultimate return to home and family by claiming that "it's for the children," but really, he returns because he lacks the strength to stand alone, in the right.

Flynn argues that although Mindon recognizes the meaninglessness of his life, he returns to it because he loves it nevertheless (73). This argument seems to be a facile one; the depth of Mindon's rationalization process may allow him to think that he loves his home, but the juxtaposition of the more overt ironic commentary of Wharton's observer narrator, and the covert irony of Mindon's inner justifications of everyone, including himself, cast doubt on his ability to love his life, or to love anything. Certainly, in returning to this life, he reveals that he does not or cannot love himself, and it is this, perhaps, that makes Mindon an object of our sympathy or pity, however fleetingly, as well as an object of our scorn.

Both the stories "The Angel at the Grave" (1901) and "The Descent of Man" (1904) move away from the theme of marriage to examine the variance between the lofty heights of the intellectual or academic, and the noisy emotional world of popular culture. Wharton ruthlessly scrutinizes the differences between one realm and the other; but more significantly she reveals through covert stable irony the ramifications of the popularizing and sentimentalizing of what had been serious philosophical ideas. It is this "translation downward" of serious ideas that

Wharton, herself an intellectual, despises in the writing of so many of her predecessors and contemporaries, thus informing her ironic stance.

Further contributing to this stance is Wharton's friendship with Sally Norton, upon whom the story of Paulina Anson is based (Benstock 112). Like Paulina, Sally had a chance to marry, but instead chose to serve as her father's (Charles Elliot Norton) assistant until his death, later editing his letters (112). Sally Norton was one of Wharton's closest female friends at the time she was writing "The Angel at the Grave," and thus fictionalized as Paulina, is subject to both sympathy and scorn (112). In the story Wharton presents us with another parody of heredity theory through the unfortunate and predestined Paulina Anson, whose family inheritance is to maintain her grandfather's high intellectual status, disregarding the more sentimental tastes and interests of the public that initially venerated him. The observer narrator tells us that Paulina's entire identity is not dependent upon her unique qualities, but was formed by the shadow of the great philosopher, her grandfather Orestes Anson. "She had been born, as it were, into a museum, and cradled in a glass case with a label; the first foundations of her consciousness being built on the rock of her grandfather's celebrity" (Wharton 245). This initial image of Paulina encased, labeled and determined by her predecessors becomes the point of departure for the stable, covert ironic speculation of the observer narrator. Orestes is her "hero," the dominant personality of her life and that of the aunts who raised her. The observer early resorts to a fairly overt sarcasm when describing these two aunts. They are not "intellectuals" but conventional women of average intellects and predictable tastes, who can recite portions of sentimental poetry, or copy "selections" in copper plate, but who lack true appreciation for Orestes' complex and lofty ideas. If "respiration was difficult on the cloudy heights of metaphysic," then these two women were asthmatic (246). On Orestes himself the observer turns his ironic gaze; he has reached "intellectual pre-eminence" based on the coincidence of inferior (as Wharton would judge it) public taste: aesthetic judgement based on "emotion," eschewing anything remotely European or English. Here is a world in which intellectualism is superficial: "Historians who were 'getting up' the period" would consult Paulina, as would "ladies with inexplicable yearnings" who would plead "for an interpretation of phrases which had 'influenced' them, but which they had not quite understood" (Wharton 248). The single quotation marks in this passage indicate the observer-narrator's ironic disdain for such pseudo-intellectuals to whom Paulina yields her expertise. As Carol Singley, in *Matters of Mind and Spirit* suggests, Wharton takes the ironic position of the "cold rationalist" in her observer-narrator's treatment of Paulina as her defense against such sentimentality (51). Being labeled emotional, and thus "feminine" would have denied her serious treatment, typical of the patriarchal tradition of female "service" to the "masculine genius" that Wharton, through her irony, rejects (52). To his admiring public, Orestes Anson's personal daily habits are more interesting than his philosophic stance. The observer is scornful both of the public who finds it "interesting to know" what the philosopher "eats for breakfast," and of the children whose filial loyalty promulgates such information (Wharton 246). The narrator's tone here provides us with the most overt stable irony in this story, offering scathing commentary throughout.

Most pointedly ironic is the observer's use of religious language: poor Paulina becomes the inheritor of "the family temple" where her grandfather, as its local divinity, is worshipped; narratorial sarcasm underscores the sense that this divinity is self-bestowed and undeserving. But unlike her aunts, who inherit the shrine out of mere family connection, Paulina is deemed even worthier of her post because of her "exceptional intelligence" (247). We see here a repeated reference to predetermination, destiny and fate. Barbara White suggests that this theme of destiny represents Wharton's working out of personal issues, especially those of a female artist and her rebellion against such fate or destiny (54).

In these opening paragraphs and throughout the story Wharton's observer narrator underscores the absurdity of four women dedicating their lives to the promotion of Orestes' greatness. The narrator continually makes an analogy between the house in which Orestes lived and the idea of a temple or shrine, or some public place of worship. To emphasize this analogy even further, and to indicate to us that there is a discrepancy between what these women believe about Orestes, represented by the house, and the way they actually live their lives founded on these beliefs, the house is always personified, via capitalization: the "House possessed her" (Wharton 249). As D.B. Flynn notes, the house is what provides Paulina with the parameters of an identity she lacks: "it stood for a monument of ruined civilizations, and its white portico opened on legendary distances" (Flynn 93, Wharton 247). Its walls, covered in crayon portraits, provide Paulina with "historic scenery" when to others and certainly to the audience "the cold spotless thinly-furnished interior might have suggested the shuttered mind of a maiden lady who associates fresh air and sunlight with dust and discoloration" (247). Yet Paulina's intelligence renders her the "interpreter of the oracle," the "high priestess" of the shrine. There is a discrepancy between how Paulina is taught to see herself, as the hereditary and rightful keeper of the shrine and the "priestess" of his "temple," and what she is, in fact just another "maiden lady" with a "shuttered mind" in a long line of such women. This provides us early on with an ironic statement that is only technically covert in that Wharton does not spell it out for us with a direct announcement of irony (247, 248).

The irony of Paulina's situation is sensible to most readers immediately, and were that all to the story, just the unfolding of this nominally covert discrepancy, the story would be a failure indeed. But from this standpoint, the story's "happy" ending, often derided as representing a resignation to patriarchy is entirely necessary. [1] It is doubly ironic in that Paulina thinks that it is her choice to

---

[1] See Barbara White, *Edith Wharton: A Study of the Short Fiction* 1991, p. 54

stay; she doesn't see that her remaining in the service of her father is predestined. This is not the first time that she has chosen so. Hewlett Winsloe, her rejected suitor, is an unexpected surprise to readers, not only in that Paulina would have been at all interested in him, but that the story does not detail the struggle of choosing between her suitor and her grandfather. Had Faulkner written this story, this struggle of choosing between one who is vital and ardent and one who is a dead but domineering presence in Paulina's life would have been the story itself. But in Wharton's conception of Paulina, the inexplicable ease of the choice, the fact of its end result, and not the process through which it was achieved, is crucial to the ironic stance she takes towards Paulina. The observer mockingly parallels Paulina's "moment over the black guilt of temptation" to marry Winsloe and be swept off to an Ansonless New York, to Persephone, "snatched from the warm fields of Enna, peer[ing] half-consentingly down the abyss that opened at her feet" (249). But Paulina is utterly overwhelmed and determined by "the ghosts of dead duties walking unappeased," by the "disapproval as reached her" not from living people, but, again, from "the walls of the house" itself, which "possessed her" and "imposed a conqueror's claim," and thus must refuse Winsloe (249). Thus Winsloe's lack of awareness of "the shadowy claim" of Orestes over her life is his kiss goodbye. With grim irony, the observer narrator shows us the futility of this choice, but also reveals its desolateness too; we see simultaneously both irony and sympathy, as the narrative voice shifts from third person omniscient into limited narration.

Paulina, like Persephone, senses that she has a fate that she cannot change or deny. This too is surprising; unlike Mindon's position in "The Line of Least Resistance" or Delia's obliviousness until the end of "The Lamp of Psyche," Paulina seems somewhat more conscious of her position and the limitations of it. She has to "justify" it, and thus her life itself, by writing the life of Orestes (249). When Paulina takes Orestes' biography to her publisher in Boston, she recognizes that she has sacrificed her life to the writing of Orestes yet she is unable to rebel against the inevitability of her choice: "she had a sudden vision of the loneliness to which this last parting condemned her. All her youth, all her dreams, all her renunciations lay in that neat bundle on her knee: It was not so much her grandfather's life as her own that she had written" (250). The world has not waited for the great man's biography to be completed; it has moved on. Again the irony of Paulina's situation is not especially covert, but the observer narrator, while not covering the irony, is again sympathetic towards Paulina, as the narration again shifts from third person omniscient into third-person limited narration, revealing Paulina's self-questioning and self-criticism. She realizes, before the end of the story, that her self-justifications of her life have been self-delusions. Neither her grandfather nor his ideas and doctrines are immortal. When she arrives at this conclusion, she realizes the futility of the last forty years of her life:

> It seemed to her that she had been walled alive into a tomb hung with the effigies of dead ideas...It was the sense of wasted labor that oppressed her; of two lives consumed in that ruthless process that uses generations of effort to build a single cell. There was a dreary parallel between her grandfather's fruitless toil and her own unprofitable sacrifice. Each in turn had kept vigil by a corpse. (253)

Why then is Paulina again led back into worshipping at the shrine? Although Paulina recognizes the parameters of her situation, she ironically does not recognize her own need for it; this is the more covert irony in the story. George Corby and the coincidence of his arrival with a newly discovered pamphlet on the "amphioxus" are likewise covertly ironic. As Singley points out, that a forgotten transcendentalist should regain his stature visa vis the discovery of a Darwinian idea is itself ironic (*Matters of Mind and Spirit* 52); had he been alive, Orestes would have accepted fame on evolutionary terms. George Corby becomes the means by which Paulina can reevaluate her own life as she readjusts her notions of Orestes. Thus, as in "The Line of Least Resistance," we do not have a truly happy ending, but we do not have an utterly pessimistic one either. A new illusion of her grandfather replaces the old one, and the most covert irony of all is that beyond Paulina's hopefulness with which the story ends is the self-entrapment created by her eager acceptance of Corby's project. That Paulina is not only able but also willing to "reshutter" her life rather than redirect it – by exercising her free will to choose – ironically validates the entire Darwinian argument that life is determined by heredity. The hopeful Paulina, like Mindon, cannot apply to the rest of her life the lesson that the first forty years should have taught her: she is destined, fated to worship, and that "choosing" to do so does not justify the wasted years such a choice effects.

Wharton approaches the problem of popularizing science from the opposite stance in "The Descent of Man" by creating Professor Linyard, who popularizes and sentimentalizes his own scientific theories because he is seduced by the monetary rewards that popular culture can bestow. Of the two characters, Linyard is the more culpable first because he chooses his own path, while Paulina "chooses" what heredity determined she would choose. But he is also more culpable because he thinks he can exist in both the realm of the popular and the realm of the intellectual without compromise or sacrifice. By creating the "ironic joke" of his book that only he and his elite colleagues can appreciate, he thinks he has a foot in both the camps of popular and elite culture, trying to maintain his status and reputation in one, while still reaping the financial benefits of the other.

One perceptive reviewer of the story, when it first appeared in 1904, notes the complexity of the situation that Wharton has created for her character. He especially comments on her "genius" at portraying "artificial existence," in which people discover that they "are born into it [illusion] and die out of it without discovering that they have never really lived at all" (qtd. in *Contemporary Reviews* 79).[2] This is precisely the dilemma in "The Descent of Man." Linyard,

---

[2] *Independent* 56 (9 June 1904): 1334-1335.

through the publication of *The Vital Thing*, replaces one set of illusions with another, never realizing that it is he, and not his book, that is ironic.

Wharton's allusive title presents the audience with the most overt irony in the story. Wharton obviously read and studied Darwin's work, and places her more minor and ironic "Descent" within the context of the late nineteenth-century debates between science and religion, as well as between elite and popular market culture (Singley 3, Schriber 31). But immediately in the very first paragraph of the story Wharton enters her irony and her ironic character into two other arenas as well: that of his placid real life marriage versus the more volatile relationships of the romance novel. Linyard's idea for *The Vital Thing* is not merely an idea but an "adventure," and he the adventurer. Linyard is "the hero of romance" whose literary idea, unlike a real life "female," does not need to take up as much space. Rather, his love "can accommodate itself to a single molecule of the brain or expand to the circumference of the horizon," unlike "the somewhat inelastic circle of Mrs. Linyard's affections" (Wharton 347). Through her use of this observer narrator here, Wharton is able to achieve a multilayering of ironies, by offering a kaleidoscopic view of themes treated ironically, shifting in and out of the foreground of the reader's understanding.

When we first meet Linyard, we are apt to despise him; the observer narrator, in shifting our focus to the context of Linyard's marriage, voices sarcasm-laden opinions about the state of Linyard's domestic affairs, again doubling the irony by using the language of the romance novel. Linyard commits only "mental infidelities," avoiding real life "sentimental crises" by being "scrupulously careful not to shirk the practical obligations of the [marital] bond" (348). His mistress is the "universe of thought," ideas which "weav[e] their spells about him . . . this new fancy of the Professor's was simply one embodied laugh. It was, in other words, the smile of relaxation at the end of a long day's toil" (348). Linyard blames his lackluster marriage on his wife's lack of interest in ideas such as "entymology," or "the transmission of acquired characteristics" (348). His role in the marriage, much like Mindon's, is therefore "impersonal"; his ideas "had to support his family" financially, while emotionally he is "indifferent" (348-349). Difficult though it is to support his family as a scientist he does so out of a dim sense of "paternal obligation" (349). The observer-narrator's dry report of Linyard's attitudes towards his family sharply contrasts the much more lyrical, emotional, quasi-religious language with which he describes Linyard's relationship to science. Science is an "inaccessible goddess" who resides in "the orchard of forbidden knowledge" (349). The draw of that which is forbidden and therefore exciting recalls again the sensationalism of the romance novel. Real life, as represented by his family, is for Linyard "a narrow strip of homespun woven in a monotonous pattern" but his mistress, science, is an "enchanted region" with "color and substance" (348).

However, as time progresses, the real financial demands of Linyard's family bear down upon him. He realizes that the gap between his wife's world and his own has narrowed and science has become interesting to the "larger public":

> Everyone now read scientific books and expressed an opinion on them. The ladies and the clergy had taken them up first; now they had passed to the schoolroom and the kindergarten. Daily life was regulated on scientific principles; the daily papers had their 'scientific jottings'; nurses passed examinations in hygienic science and babies were fed and dandled according to the new psychology. (349)

Here too, as in "The Angel at the Grave," the observer narrator's sarcastic stance towards the public's taste for rarefied ideas, so long as they are easily digestible, is not especially covert. The narrator's discussion of popularized science as a "false goddess" who would sell herself, "offer[ing] her charms in the marketplace" drips with scorn (350). Initially, Linyard views this goddess, his mistress, as the true one, and thinks that he could nobly "avenge" her by writing a satire. He sees himself as the romance hero, rescuing his lover. But he has no inkling of the contradiction he enters as he writes and prepares to sell his "'popular scientific book'" (350). His book would demonstrate his "superior knowledge to abound in the sense of the ignorant, [so] that even the gross crowd would join in the laugh against its augurs" (350).

Linyard's satire, however, is so complete that it even fools his old college friend and would-be publisher Ned Harviss, who, to both Linyard's delight and dismay, has taken the book seriously, missing the irony completely. This confusion is what convinces Linyard to agree to Harviss' next idea, to sell the book "as a genuine thing" and to "catch a big public" as well as a big profit (354). And here, as in "The Angel at the Grave," the overtly ironic observer-narrator disguises the more covert irony of the tale by moving into third person limited narration as Linyard ponders what publishing the book as a genuine thing would mean. Now he could avenge his goddess because only "the initiated" "would know at once: and however long a face he pulled his colleagues would see the tongue in his cheek" (355). Simultaneously, he would satisfy public taste: "as a profession of faith, as the recantation of an eminent biologist whose leanings had hitherto been supposed to be toward a cold determinism, it would bring in a steady income to author and publisher" (355). The fact that the book was already in press lends even more weight to Harviss' claim that as the genuine thing the book would sell. "If he had had time to think the matter over his scruples might have dragged him back; but his conscience was eased by the futility of resistance" (355). Wharton takes the opposite stance to that in "The Angel at the Grave." In the former the predestined and determined Paulina "chooses" her path to revitalize her god's status by revealing him to be an evolutionist. In "The Descent of Man" in choosing not to stop publication of a book that he has authored, but that in no way expresses his true views about religion and determinism, the determinist uses the excuse of determinism itself. He has no choice; the wheels have already begun to turn. *The Vital Thing* becomes Linyard's big payoff, leading to another, his popular "Scientific Sermons."

One critic notes, relying on Darwin's ideas about 'moral sense,' that Linyard's "fall" may be determined by the "social 'tyrants' of the understandable desire for societal rewards of public popularity and financial profit" (Schribner 31-33). However the most covert irony of all in the story is that while Linyard applauds himself for the success of the satire, which has fooled and garnered profits from a lesser public, he himself satisfies the very same public taste – he allows himself to become a popular public figure: "Admiring readers learned the name of the only breakfast food in use at his table, of the ink with which 'The Vital Thing' had been written, the soap with which the author's hands were washed…his head passed in due course from the magazine and the newspaper to the biscuit tin and the chocolate box" (Wharton 360). Linyard, beginning with a popular book, but a book nonetheless, falls by his own choice from the realm of popular print culture to the level of popular market culture. No longer the seat of ideas, his "head" represents crass consumerism of biscuits and chocolates; he has become the very false deity he sought to revenge, selling himself happily on the marketplace to whomever would buy him. The covert irony turns in on itself, for what is at the outset the motivator for ironic interpretation, popular taste, becomes the motivator for un-ironic interpretation. The intellectual Linyard has been "Ansonized," detached from the very ideas, false though they initially might have been, that put him in the public eye to begin with. Covertly ironic is that in this way Wharton questions the nature of irony, and the intent to be ironic; it questions the value of interpretation, a question obviously important to Wharton's own status as a writer. Brown argues that this story illustrates Wharton's fascination with irony itself, making rhetorical irony the actual subject of the story: "the theme, its slipperiness and the title, though somewhat opaque (and clearly allusive) suggests that an inability to perceive irony hearkens the decline of humanity" (Brown 22). The story is ultimately about the ironies inherent in an act of irony, and about seeing irony everywhere but in oneself, which is precisely what Linyard fails to do (23,24).

A further covert irony Wharton executes through Linyard has to do with the fact that Linyard's "scientific Sermons" series is something he writes for a woman's weekly (Schriber 34). Not only does Wharton, in "The Angel at the Grave," and in "The Descent of Man," take a stab at the patriarchal stance that deems women and their writing emotional, sentimental, and therefore inferior; she also criticizes popular fiction in general, even as she empowers the women who crave it because they control the market for it. Mary Schriber notes that the reading public for whom Linyard writes is female, and therefore, women determine his success or failure (34). Linyard's increasing public appearances create in him an enjoyment of female praise: "Not that the Professor inspired, or sought to inspire, sentimental emotions; but he expanded in the warm atmosphere of personal interest which some of his new acquaintances contrived to create about him. It was delightful to talk of serious things in a setting of frivolity, and to be personal without being domestic" (359). The observer-narrator's matter-of-fact dismissal of Linyard's marriage and relationship with his wife as "impersonal," as merely an obligation from which he can "free" himself by continuing to market himself is in stark contrast with the "personal" and "delightful" mingling of women and "serious things" he experiences when making his public appearances. Linyard replaces his former mistress, "the universe of ideas," with another: the utterly undemanding yet thoroughly enjoyable idea of a "third type of woman," so different from his wife, whose financial demands of him give him only a "negative satisfaction" (359).

Does Professor Linyard show weakness in succumbing yet again to the draw of popular market culture at the end of the story, or can we excuse him because the lure is too great? His proposal of writing a "serious" book in his "'old line'" of "what Harviss scathingly calls " 'beetles and so forth'" is met with skepticism; these serious ideas are now the side benefits of financial success, the "harmless amusement" he may "permit himself" when not writing something that sells (362). Consoling himself that " ' it's only putting it off for six months'" and that he will now be able to buy better instruments for his real work, Linyard allows himself to agree to another book deal in the popular vein. While one may argue that the temptation of another fat check brings about his fall, the lure of more money doesn't lead directly to his descent; rather, familial demands do so. Far easier is it for Linyard, as he sees it, to placate Mrs. Linyard and his children by giving in to the force of consumerism, in order to satisfy their monetary demands.

Underlying the relatively overt irony of a man giving in to the thing he has initially sworn to oppose is the double irony of doing so because of an apathetic and unfulfilling marriage with which he is content: "the Professor was not an unkind man. He really enjoyed making his family happy, and it was his own business if his reward for doing so was that it kept them out of his way" (359). The vague allure of his new mistress to our hero is that she is not any one real woman, so he need not throw all caution to the winds for her and overturn the status quo in order to have her. Like Mindon, Linyard gives us a dim view of the potential for meaningful personal relationships. The real descent in the story is the descent of love to mere duty. Linyard is utterly oblivious of the grim reality of his marital situation, and is without any real desire to use his financial windfall to change it, just so he is left to ponder his mistress alone and in peace. With this story Wharton reveals a grimly ironic stance towards marriage and the promulgation of the human species for its improvement, since nothing for Linyard has actually improved; he doesn't realize that he should even wish it to.

If "The Descent of Man" is about someone not only unable to make a change in his marital status but one who is unaware that one may even be beneficial, "The Reckoning" is just the opposite. Not only does Wharton deal with the ramifications, socially and psychologically, of divorce in this story, but she also questions how a person can learn that such a change is, in fact, necessary (White 160). The observer narrator's ironic voice borders on nastiness early in the story. Through this voice Wharton criticizes the pseudo-intellectualism and pseudo-aestheticism of the socially elite that the Westalls gently exploit: the "mentally unemployed" need "their brain food cut up for them" – nothing in Westall's talks on "the New Ethics" must be too provocative or complex (Wharton 420). Mrs. Van Sideren, sponsor of the series of talks, dresses up her otherwise dull and ordinary drawing room functions with an easel, whiskey and soda. Such bohemian touches allow her to suggest "artiness" without actually being artistic. The observer-narrator quips that Mrs. Van Sideren "almost wish[es]" that her husband could paint (420). The ironic significance of the word 'almost' is unmistakable and poignant: the observer narrator tells us that these are people who would disdain producing real art, and tacitly, Wharton revenges herself upon her family's and society's implied disdain of her artistic endeavors. To further this aim, the smirking observer narrator aligns art with "conduct": "a teacher who pronounced marriage immoral was somehow as distinguished as a painter who depicted purple grass and a green sky. The Van Sideren set were tired of the conventional color scheme in art and conduct" (421).

It is here that the observer provides us with the first irony in the story: the Westalls move with a group of people who value an art not for its intrinsic beauty and value, but rather for the very fact of its unconventionality. Green skies are to be lauded as an artistic breakthrough simply because they break with the convention of painting them blue, and for no other reason. Similarly they value discussions of "new ethics" and the "immorality of marriage," not because they believe these ideas to be of worth, but rather because they too are unconventional. But, the observer implicitly challenges, how would this group feel about the application of these unconventional morals to their own lives? Julia Westall becomes the test case for these principles that defined her marriage.

The first section of the story establishes a change in Julia's attitude towards her husband's open discussion of their doctrine on marriage. Like Linyard, Clement Westall is "hawking his convictions at the street corner," which to Julia's mind, is "vulgar" (421). But unlike Linyard, Westall believes utterly in what he publicly proclaims. Although these doctrines were originally hers, she now dislikes their public expression. Here, Julia voices a somewhat old-fashioned notion of what is and is not appropriate for young girls like Una Van Sideren to hear. Had Una been her daughter, Julia certainly would not have allowed her to mix with such company: "the girl had no business to be there. It was 'horrid' – Mrs. Westall found herself slipping back into the old feminine vocabulary – simply 'horrid' to think of a young girl's being allowed to listen to such talk" (421). However, the observer-narrator, foreshadowing the covert irony inherent later in the story, does not allow Julia to get away with this assessment of her soon-to-be rival. "The fact that Una smoked cigarettes and sipped an occasional cocktail did not in the least tarnish a certain radiant innocence which made her appear the victim, rather than the accomplice, of her parent's vulgarities" (421). Here the observer-narrator mocks this change in attitude, by pointing out that Julia's perspective is rather rose-tinted.

What brings about Julia's initial ideas about marriage, and colors her perspective now? Wharton uses architectural interiors once again to represent emotional interiors. Julia's first marriage, we learn, was as conventional as the "wilderness of rosewood and upholstery" in which "she had never been able to establish any closer relation than between a traveler and a railway station" (423). But "the room for which she had left the other room," and the husband for whom she had left another, are now both "strange" and "unfamiliar" (423). When she divorces John Arment, no one is much scandalized; the unconventional choice she makes is almost quiet, socially agreed upon as necessary, because Arment is "impossible." He is intrinsically selfish, but socially impossible to put up with. Thus, Julia develops the philosophy that when people outgrow or injure each other, they may leave the relationship with impunity:

> That was what divorce was for: . .the only necessary condition to a harmonious marriage was a frank recognition of this truth, and a solemn agreement between the contracting parties to keep faith with themselves, and not to live together for a moment after complete accord had ceased to exist between them. The new adultery was unfaithfulness to self. (427)

Her remarriage is, then, merely "an unimportant concession to social prejudice" because convention still required the ceremony. Would she have agreed to live with Westall without it? Could she have ever really been a character like Lydia, in "Souls Belated"? For Julia easily says that ceremony simply bows to social convention, since in her mind she redefines what a marriage is: "now that the door of divorce stood open, no marriage need be an imprisonment, and the contract therefore no longer involved any diminution of self respect" (427). Perhaps this is so, but Julia oversimplifies the issue; the ease of her divorce belies the complexity of relationships in general, in which there must be a personal investment or compromise that her doctrine denies is necessary.

There is irony, retrospectively, in Una's complimentary summation of Westall's talks, for the "freer expansion of the individual – the law of fidelity to one's self" parrots Julia's former mantra and is therefore overtly ironic (426). That this claim becomes Westall's justification for leaving Julia for Una is a more covert irony. However, this doctrine of the primacy of the self was embodied by Julia's first husband, and is why she rejects him: "John Arment was impossible, but the sting of his impossibility lay in the fact that he made it impossible for those about him to be other than himself...he had excluded from the world everything of which he did not feel a personal need: had become, as it were, a climate in which only his own requirements survived" (426). Julia leaves John because of his pervasive, pesky egocentricity, by which she had been "bruis[ed]...and wounded in every fiber of her spirit" (426-427). Thus the observer narrator leads us through a maze of recursive, and therefore increasingly covert ironies: Julia turns John's insistent primacy of self into the doctrine by which she justifies her leaving him for Westall. This in turn becomes the very doctrine by which Westall then validates his ending of their marriage, and which Una unconsciously echoes, foreshadowing for us and for Julia (hence Julia's "wandering resentment" of Una) Una's new role in Westall's life (421).

The observer narrator in this story, while nastily ironic in the beginning of the story, is notably quiet as the limited narration reveals Julia's perplexity. The observer's lack of irony here is the most covert irony of all: Julia's earnestness and sincere confusion in the middle of the story suggests that it is she whom the observer-narrator targets. She is utterly unconscious of the irony of her own situation, which is about to boomerang upon her.

Julia doesn't entirely lack self-awareness, though. She admits that her ideas have changed in practice, if not in theory: "He and she were one, one in the mystic sense which alone gave marriage its significance. The new law was not for them, but for the disunited creatures forced into a mockery of union. The gospel she had felt called on to proclaim had no bearing on her own case" (428). That Julia would revert to conventional notions of marriage while thinking specifically of her own marriage is not surprising; traditional mores are internally entrenched, however strongly one may outwardly reject them (Singley 63-64). But Julia never counted on falling in love, and on wanting to be married, in the full, albeit old-fashioned sense of the word. Thus, even though she knows that she must make this change in attitude known to Clement Westall, she hedges, speaking in hints and fragments, and breaking off at the most crucial points. Ironically, it is Westall who, much like Corbett in "The Lamp of Psyche," immediately understands his wife's dilemma, and who voices it when she cannot: " 'You *have* ceased to take this view, then?' he said as she broke off. 'you no longer believe that husbands and wives *are* justified in separating -- under such conditions?....the doctrine having served your purpose when you needed it, you now repudiate it" (Wharton 429). That it is he and not she who recognizes her hypocrisy is telling. He is at first unwilling to "proclaim himself a follower of the new creed," and is the "moral coward" in Julia's mind who once failed "to live up to the convictions for which their marriage was supposed to stand" (421). Yet it is he who does not "repudiate" the doctrine, but views it with conviction as "'a complete justification of the course'" he is about to take, namely, leaving her for Una (430). Critics agree that ultimately Juila's inner doctrine becomes her imprisonment, and that she becomes the victim of her own marriage (Fracasso 28-32, Singley 64).

Finally, in the third section of the story, as the irony of her situation becomes fully known to Julia, the observer-narrator is again un-ironic, allowing Julia herself to generate irony upon irony:

> the law itself would side with her, would defend her. The law? What claim had she upon it? She was the prisoner of her own choice: she had been her own legislator, and she was the predestined victim of the code she had devised . . . She was the victim of the theories she renounced. It was as though some giant machine of her own making had caught her up in its wheels and was grinding her to atoms. (Wharton 431-432).

Julia's reliance on such determinist and victimist imagery divorces her from intention, and therefore from responsibility as she sees it. She only acknowledges years after the fact that divorcing John on the grounds of who he is "had been cruel" and that she must tell him so. Julia recognizes this truth, and that the definitions of conventionality and unconventionality are meaningless without "an inner law . . . the obligation that love creates...being loved as well as loving" (436). Here too a descent occurs, though one of a slightly different nature: the mutually obligating love she feels for her husband is no longer possible within the parameters of relationships as Julia has redefined them. "The Reckoning" becomes another story in which the husband is a person with whom the wife cannot come to easy terms, especially because of her complicity in making him who he is. And like "The Lamp of Psyche," we see here a story about Julia's recognition, ultimately, of her own illusions and limitations, her own hypocrisy and complicity in the outcome of her and her husbands' lives. The "reckoning" or payback for living and behaving unconventionally and retrospectively justifying it with a doctrine is that others will then live by or apply them too. Ultimately, the irony extends beyond the merely situational: overtly ironic is that Westall applies the lesson that Julia insisted on teaching him, and leaves her. Covertly, she learns that she does not believe in the very doctrine by which she has tried to live; Julia makes the discovery that she is as conventional with respect to marriage as the next person, but she cannot see this self-illusion until, ironically, she is married no longer. The ultimate irony is that she too fulfills her own philosophy, one of self that does not allow for happiness found with another. Thus Julia ends up alone, with the self she longed to free in spite of marriage, rather than because of it.

Chapter Two
The Ironic Spectator

In chapter one we examined one type of irony found in Wharton's short stories, that of an "observer" narrator who, like a god from on high, offers comments and opinions of the characters on the stage below with an ironic perspective that varies in its degree of covertness. Rarely does the observer reveal an overt irony by simply asserting an ironic perspective; when he does, it is often through an overtly ironic tone. But those ironies which are more covert tend to be ironies whose meanings are "stable" or "fixed." That is, they are ironies whose meanings, once reconstructed, are clear and relatively unambiguous.

In this chapter, however, we will examine a different kind of ironic perspective: one which is generated by a character we can deem the "spectator." Sometimes in first person, and sometimes in third person limited narration, the spectator reflects upon the events central to the story, watching, drawing his own conclusions. He is only a minor participant in the story's action. This narrator occupies an emotionally mediatory, objective position — or thinks himself to, and does not necessarily represent Wharton herself as directly as the observer narrator seems to. Indeed, at times this spectator might be in direct and perhaps ironic opposition to Wharton herself, generating another covert irony in the story. Stories in this group have ironies that are covert and somewhat stable, but not necessarily fixed or local, because we receive them through the inherently biased mind of the spectator, and not the omniscient, emotionally detached mind of the observer.

Though it lacks a great deal of plot, Barbara White calls "The Other Two" (1904) one of "the best" of Wharton's stories: it is what some might call situational irony at its best as "the situation is revealed to those in it" (White 162). And, as White points out, we have little narratorial omniscience – "manners" of "dress, gesture, expression," as impressed upon our spectator's reflecting consciousness, are what reveal this situation to the characters and to us alike

(162). But is the irony in the story merely situational, created out of contrived coincidence? Many critics point to this reliance on coincidence as the story's main weakness. Although the twist of plot that brings together Alice Waythorn's three husbands is contrived, it carries us straight towards an "accumulation of ironies," as M. M. Brown puts it (Brown 50). Irony is Wharton's conscious choice, not a mere technique, but rather is a means of revealing some greater "'human significance,'" as Wharton herself claims in *A Backward Glance*.

The question then becomes, what significance, or rather, whose, is challenged and revealed in this humorous outcome of a social dilemma that society could not yet account for? Here, as in "The Reckoning," Wharton looks at divorce, and comments upon the disparity between the law and society. In the former story, as we have discussed, Wharton shows us a character that justifies her legal action after the fact with a personal philosophy. Julia's ideas about the freedom of a "new" marriage do not in any way account for the emotional bonds one might form; the relative legal ease of divorce belies the emotional difficulties one might have prior to the legal action.

In this story, however, Wharton attacks the issue of divorce from the opposite stance: how does one, after the fact, deal with the tenuous but still existing emotional bonds between people no longer legally bound? Waythorn, meeting Alice's first husband Haskett face-to-face, rightly comments that "the law had not obligingly removed all difficulties in the way of their meeting" (Wharton 388). Although legally there is no embarrassing relationship left between Alice and her ex-husbands, the fact of their past relationships cannot be erased by any court of law. Wharton not only questions the social consequences of divorce, as Waythorn wonders how he is to behave and to speak to Alice's former husbands, but Wharton also ponders the personal consequences as well. How will this awkward social contact between Waythorn and Haskett, interminable since there is a child involved, affect Waythorn's self-proclaimed "unstable sensibilities" (380)? "Waythorn was an idealist. He always refused to recognize unpleasant contingencies till he found himself confronted with them, and then he saw them followed by a spectral chain of consequences. His next days were thus haunted, and he determined to try to lay the ghosts by conjuring them up in his wife's presence" (391). Never being confronted by the real Mr. Haskett, Waythorn has been able to pretend that such a figure, and therefore such a past, never existed; his wife's physical presence in Waythorn's life should be able to remove any thought of the past that Haskett represents. But when he confronts Alice, her only concern is that Haskett, despite his legal claims to his daughter, is socially inappropriate. "'It is very ungentlemanly of him,'" to make his objections to Lily's French governess known, she cries immediately, and "'it's not as if he could ever be a help to Lily'" financially or socially (391). Waythorn is quite disturbed that Alice would place his own much better social position ahead of Haskett's legal rights as Lily's father. Wharton, through Waythorn, shows us that the complexity of legal relationships has not yet been absorbed by social custom: "Waythorn . . . even guessed in the latter a mild contempt for such advantages as his relation with the Waythorns might offer. Haskentt's sincerity of purpose made him invulnerable, and his successor had to accept him as a lien on the property" (392). Waythorn, previously, has been used to thinking of the world and being thought of by it in the economic terms by which his society is determined: one either has or has not, owns or owns not; he is thrown off balance by the sheer legal fact of Haskett's paternal interest. No amount of progress up the social ladder, nor the legal fact of divorce from Alice, can eradicate Haskett from his daughter's life, nor, therefore, from his own.

Wharton thus establishes her first covert irony in the story: a person who is legally divorced from another is never truly divorced emotionally from the past by virtue of his participation in it; the undeniable concrete fact of this past bond is Lily herself. But out of Waythorn's natural, if not legal, interest in Lily rises a second covert irony: his attitude towards Alice drastically changes as he encounters her first and second husbands.

Initially, Waythorn ignores the slight disparagement that society bestows on Alice for being a woman of lesser social origins: "was it in Pittsburgh or Utica? – society, while promptly accepting her, had reserved the right to cast a doubt on its own indiscrimination" (381). Alice's second marriage gives her entrée into the social set to which Waythorn belongs, and thus he "could afford to smile at these innuendoes" (381). Waythorn, relying on the business language with which he interprets his world, has "discounted" those innuendoes since "society has not yet adapted itself to the consequences of divorce, and that till the adaptation takes place every woman who uses the freedom the law accords her must be her own justification" (381). Not only do Alice's previous relationships not trouble him, he seems, at first, almost proud of them, and of her for "surmounting obstacles without seeming to be aware of them" (381). Satisfied, he sees her nature as "richer, warmer," as "charming" and "engaging," and labels her as a loving, affectionate mother (380-381).

But immediately, as we receive these impressions of her through Waythorn's reflecting consciousness, he begins to modify, covertly and ever so slightly, this view. Lily has been gravely ill, but Alice has "the perfectly balanced nerves" of a young child; "no woman ever wasted less tissue in unproductive worry" (380). And while this is at first a virtue, it will not remain so for long. When she appears at dinner, she is "nearly worried" (380). How important is this one word, "nearly." With this one word we begin to detect a slight censure of her behavior. Waythorn, not yet consciously, begins to see her as less than utterly devoted to her daughter: she is almost worried, not yet in a state of worry when most parents would be. This is a slight distinction, but one necessary to understanding Waythorn's changing view of Alice, and the irony inherent in it; he would rather she be worried, but not show her worry. But when he tells her to "'try to forget about it,'" "it" being Haskett's imminent arrival, Waythorn sees that she has, in fact, forgotten it, and her forgetting hypocritically troubles him. "In a moment or two their eyes met above the sparkling glasses. Her own were quite clear and untroubled: he saw that she had obeyed his injunction and forgotten" (393). The unstated and thus covert implication of this matter-of-fact observation is that Alice should not, as a caring parent who was once married to her child's father, have entirely forgotten. Some of her previous concern for Lily, had it been authentic (which the word "nearly" suggests that it was not) should have been outwardly visible. That is, he speaks the words custom demands: "put your troubles out of your mind," never expecting that she really would.

Similarly, Waythorn finds her "singularly soft and girlish appearance" the next day, after he has encountered her other ex-husband Varick on business, less charming than he would have a day earlier. With each encounter with one of Alice's former husbands, Waythorn sees her differently, and increasingly less positively. Here again, he reveals this covert irony in the language of money: it is he who "has," and the other two who "have not." Waythorn, reflecting on her girlish grace, "feel[s] himself yielding again to the joy of possessorship. They were his, those white hands with their flitting motions, his the light haze of hair, the lips and eyes" (386). But he is rudely awakened from his reverie when Alice pours cognac into his after-dinner coffee, Varick's drink, not his. This action becomes proof positive to us that, in fact, Alice will never belong entirely to him, if we can say that she has ever belonged to anyone at all.

Waythorn, however, does not immediately come to this realization; he is later offended when he learns that Alice has actually spoken "in society" to Varick because she thought that it would be "less awkward" (393). Just as he cannot own or dictate her past, he cannot determine her present either. Thus Waythorn begins to understand "the grim irony" of Alice's situation as a "social problem" where none had previously existed. Waythorn focuses on his own "sickened reaction," and rather cruelly, he evaluates her tendency to "evade difficulties or to circumvent them":

> Waythorn saw how the instinct had developed. She was 'as easy
> as an old shoe' – a shoe that too many feet had worn. Her
> elasticity was the result of tension in too many different directions.

> Alice Haskett Alice Varick – Alice Waythorn – she had been each
> in turn, and had left hanging to each name a little of her privacy, a
> little of her personality, a little of the inmost self where the
> unknown god abides. (393)

Yet again Waythorn uses the language of commercial ownership, later comparing her to a company in which he "held so many shares in his wife's personality" and in which "his predecessors were his partners in the business" (393). What is interesting here is this very role as the spectator with which he endows himself. Waythorn observes her and the other two to whom she had been married, and passes judgement, not on her "blunders" for not "resisting Hasket" nor for "yielding to Varick," but for her "acquiescence and her tact" (393). She overcomes the social awkwardness that he cannot, by falling back on superficial custom, circumventing the unpleasant social vacuum that divorce creates (393). But Waythorn takes "refuge in the cheap revenge of satirizing the situation," in economic terms: "If he paid for each day's comfort with the small change of his illusions, he grew daily to value the comfort more and set less store upon the change" (393-394). Waythorn acquiesces that the "change" is not really hers but rather his own loss of illusions and change in perspective, and although he sees the irony of marriage to Alice, viewing her ironically, he keeps his participation at the level of the spectator, exempting himself from complicity, fault or involvement.

Indeed, by distancing himself from complicity in helping her to become the person he censures, Waythorn is able to view himself as superior to and distinct from Haskett and Varick. For example, when Waythorn first encounters Varick he is "glad, in the end, to appear the more self-possessed of the two," when the "embarrassing topic" of Varick's former financial troubles, which contributed to Alice's leaving him, comes up in conversation (387). Later, as Haskett goes upstairs to see Lily, Waythorn muses about him, and about their very different social and economic circumstances, noting that at least "Varick, whatever his faults, was a gentleman in the conventional, traditional sense of the term...He and Varick had the same social habits, spoke the same language, understood the same allusions" (389). Haskett, on the other hand, represents for Waythorn a stodgy middle class enigma in which he cannot fathom Alice participating. "He could see her, as Mrs. Haskett, sitting in a 'front parlor' furnished in plush...He could see her going to the theater with Haskett – or perhaps eve to a 'Church Sociable' – she in a 'picture hat' and Haskett in a black frock coat, a little creased, with the made-up tie on an elastic" (389). At this point Waythorn reveals his elitist, snobbish nature, and even when he chastises himself for "creating a fantastic effigy of her and then passing judgment on it" he excuses himself by reflecting, somewhat resentfully, that she must be a powerful force indeed, one who could will away "every gesture, every inflection, every allusion" of her former life" (390). How dare she? Her nature, he ruminates, must be "duplicitous" in the very negation or "obliteration of...self" that allows her to climb up the social ladder with each marriage: "Haskett's very inoffensiveness shed a new light on the nature of those illusions. A man would rather think that his wife had been brutalized by her first husband than that the process has been reversed" (390). Suddenly, he sees her as a ruthlessly ambitious, man-using social climber.

That Waythorn may be correct in his rather nasty assessment of how Alice Haskett could have possibly transformed herself into Alice Waythorn, social matron par excellence, is eminently clear. D. B. Flynn argues that the story is about this social transformation of self, "look[ing] at the cost of one woman's attempt to become a real person" (Flynn 155). According to Flynn, Alice undergoes a string of self-re-inventions, "obliterat[ing] those parts which have become unacceptable," thus achieving her very self-creation, paradoxically, through "self-effacement" (158). But we only learn of Alice's self-negation to achieve self through Waythorn's reflecting consciousness, and Waythorn is biased. He is as much an unreliable narrator as he would be if he were telling the story in first person, with his own voice. Waythorn directly and frequently refers

to the "grim irony" or the "placid irony" of the situation that he observes
unfolding before him. This irony, therefore, is local, and not terribly covert. It
becomes obvious to him, and therefore, once removed, to us. What is not obvious
or ironic to him is his own position, which he does not see, nor do we
immediately throughout the story. He sees himself in the role of the spectator,
when he is in fact as much of a participant in creating his wife's identity or in
being culpable for her "loss of self,' as are, as he would put it, "the other two."
The very title of the story makes Waythorn's true position covert, and covertly
forces us to see him in the spectator role as well.

Thus the most covert irony of the tale is that Waythorn, our spectator, is
no spectator at all. In the crucial coincidence with which the story closes,
Waythorn's laugh is ambiguous. Does he ultimately see himself among, and not
separate from, the others in this social conundrum, or does the story end without
Waythorn coming to some comprehension of his ironic relationship to the "other
two"? "He took the third cup" of tea that Alice offers them "with a laugh," seeing
the humor, as we do, in the situation, but this is all that the text allows us. It is
perhaps just as ironic that the story ends with this ambiguity, marking this as a
finite, and not a local irony. While providing no answer for how one is to treat
such "ex-connections," Wharton reminds us that by virtue of a past legal
connection the "others" will always have a tenuous place in a person's present,
like it or not. Yet the self-negated-recreated Alice is the only one who seems to
accept this fact; it is she who behaves with true aplomb. When no new
convention exists for such an awkward social situation, it is only Alice who
behaves as though she were in command, by acting as the perfect hostess who is
faced with three "difficult" guests. It is perhaps Wharton's ironic joke that the
censored Alice, the socially ambitious, the self-obliterating, the worn shoe, is the
one who resolves the difficulty of their respective pasts, by simply sidestepping
social custom and ignoring their relationships with her past and present. Viewed,
as she is, through the eyes of the reflector, Alice is softened compared to the

harsher portraiture that Wharton gives to a similar social climber, Undine Spragg in *The Custom of the Country* in 1913, the same year that her own divorce becomes finalized. Alice repeatedly sheds her identity but preserves her dignity in a way that the three men, ever conscious of their relationships past and present, cannot.

The story "The Last Asset," published in 1908, seems at first glance to be a shortened version of the previously published *The House of Mirth*, or even a precursor to *The Custom of the Country*. In this story, as well as within these two novels, Wharton reveals how women driven to maintain their social status while lacking financial status, might use everyone, including the innocent nouveau riche, to provide themselves with the necessary financial support to maintain said social status. Both Undine Spragg and Lily Bart, for example, reach a point of desperation when their finances will not meet the lifestyle that requires them. But Wharton treats the three respective protagonists differently; in *The House of Mirth,* Lily's love for Selden, coupled with her innate morality, distinguish her from the cold ruthlessness of an Undine Spragg or a Mrs. Newell. In *The Custom of the Country,* Wharton demonstrates thoroughly the risks of a social climber who always fancies that there are another few rungs on the ladder still to be climbed. Undine lacks inner reflection, always justifying her course of action by claiming that her current situation is "horrid" compared to how her life would be if she could achieve the change – of dress, location, or husband – she craves.

In "The Last Asset," however, Wharton dispenses with revealing the costliness of maintaining a position at the top of the social heap. Rather, she presents us with the story of one social triumph in the career of such a woman. The knowing Mrs. Newell, anxious to socially "renovate" herself by pulling off the unlikely marriage of her daughter to a "Compte," differs from Undine Spragg in that she is utterly self-aware. Her ambitious social hunger, and her means of fulfilling it are clear to herself, if not to everyone else. We meet Mrs. Newell through the reflecting consciousness of Garnett, who comments upon Mrs.

Newell's honesty and forthright demeanor: "there was a splendid directness about Mrs. Newell. It would never have occurred to her to pretend to Garnett that she had summoned him for the pleasure of his company"(599). She uses everyone, but never pretends, as does Undine, that she is doing otherwise. Thus she summons Garnett once again to her side, as she has done for many years, and entrusts him to deliver Mr. Newell, absent this many years, to her daughter's wedding.

In Garnett we have a true spectator: he is not a part of the central action of the story – bringing about the wedding – although it is through him that Mrs. Newell achieves her ends and reels in the reluctant Mr. Newell. When we first meet Garnett, he is eating and conversing with the "old gentleman" whose name he has never bothered to learn, but which will soon be revealed as the absent Mr. Newell. Garnett, initially, is as "impersonal" as the old gentleman himself, enjoying the company of a man without needing to enter into a more intimate kind of inquiry. He is the ultimate spectator, one who is content to watch and comment, but who is unwilling to get involved on a more personal level. He notes to himself that he "had always foreseen that Mrs. Newell might someday ask him to do something he should greatly dislike" and "had simply felt that if he allowed his acquaintance with her to pass from spectatorship to participation he must be prepared to find himself, at any moment, in a queer situation" (601). Garnett relishes his spectator role, and resents any further or deeper obligation that, as he puts it, would put him "in holes so tight that there might not be room for a wriggle" (601). He relies on a mutual "casual intimacy" in which Mrs. Newell's use of him is merely expedient at that moment.

This is not the only reason, however, that Garnett endeavors to "assert" his "independence" and refuse her. Even though she is usually "direct," Garnett senses that Mrs. Newell has lied to him about the coincidence of "the little legacy from an aunt in Elmira" that is enabling Hermione to marry (598). Garnett's vague feeling is confirmed with the arrival of the Baron Schenkelderff, which "deepened the disgust with which . . . he yielded to the conviction that the Baron was Mrs. Newell's 'aunt'" (601). Mrs. Newell is trying to entangle him in her web, and it is a web tainted with the hint of impropriety in her relationship with the Baron. Mrs. Newell's story of the aunt's legacy also serves to alert Garnett to the depth of her need. The Baron's "alliance with Mrs. Newell," as Garnett later conjectures, "was doubtless a desperate attempt at rehabilitation, a forlorn hope on both sides, but likely to be an enduring tie because it represented to both partners, their last chance of escape from social extinction" (607).

This is the main difference between Lily Bart, who almost finds her "baron" in the figure of Rosedale, and Mrs. Newell: Lily has some scruples, some delicacy, whereas Mrs. Newell is willing to use her very own daughter to achieve her social ends. "What was the use of producing and educating a handsome daughter if she did not, in some more positive way, contribute to her parent's advancement?"(596). Mrs. Newell's ruthless, aggressive ambition matches Undine Spragg's. Through Garnett, Wharton even uses the same military language in this story as she does occasionally in *The Custom of the Country* to describe Mrs. Newell's compelling force. She is like an "invading army without a base of supplies" who will eventually "gain her point" and "disarm" "her foes" while not able to remember "by what means her victory had been won" (593,612). Mrs. Newell becomes almost a caricature of Wharton's more in-depth Lily and Undine. As Flynn notes, "irony surrounds the marriage in this story as Wharton exposes the machinations necessary to make it possible" (46). That Mrs. Newell should gain her point and succeed in using those around her to their best advantage is a given; the irony of her victory is apparent in Garnett's use of the title in the conclusion of the story. "Garnett himself" is "the humble instrument adjusting the different parts of the complicated machinery, and her husband, finally, as the last stake in her game, the last asset on which she could draw to rebuild her fallen fortunes" (615). For a woman to whom money is everything and yet is the one thing she lacks, even discarded husbands have their uses, and

Garnett reluctantly and ironically admires her willingness to use even the obscure Mr. Newell:

> That he had been dropped overboard at an early stage in the lady's career seemed probable...but he now saw how he had underrated his friend's faculty for using up the waste material of life. She had always struck him as the most extravagant of women, yet it turned out that by a miracle of thrift she had for years kept a superfluous husband on the chance that he might someday be useful. The day had come. (601)

In a world in which women, and not men, are objects to be disposed of as their husbands, fathers or brothers see fit, Mrs. Newell, without becoming any less feminine, has reversed the convention, overthrown the norm, and turned her husband into the object to be used, making herself the unapologetic user. What, then, saves this story from being merely an overtly ironic caricature?

Garnett acts both as an intermediary between Mrs. Newell and her husband, and as an intermediary between us and the transparent irony of the plot itself. Garnett's unwillingness to play this role is interesting; it bothers him that she would go to the extremes that she does to achieve her social ends, and the Baron's involvement disturbs him when the Hubbards' does not. Garnett, to justify his own participation in this scheme, erects a moral purpose: "It made Garnett shiver to think of her [Hermione] growing old between her mother and Schenkelderff, or such successors of the baron's as might probably attend on Mrs. Newell's waning fortunes" (603). Garnett, taking a more participatory role, sees himself as a romance "hero" saving Hermione, a "damsel in distress."

> The very inequality of the contest stirred in his blood, and made him vow that in this case, at least, the sins of the parents should not be visited on the children . . .That Hermione's marriage was a mere stake in their game did not in the least affect Garnett's view of its urgency. . .If it made of her a mere pawn in their hands, it would put her, so Garnett hoped, beyond further risk of such base uses; and to achieve this had become a necessity to him. (607)

Garnett sees, and allows us to see the covert irony that although contacting Mr.

Newell will achieve Mrs. Newell's unscrupulous end, it will, nevertheless, remove Hermione from being so used again, and give her very real happiness. And even more covertly ironic, it allows the private and sardonic Garnett himself to become involved on an emotional level, to have a very real participatory role in the family drama he was called upon to watch from afar, once his part in it has been played.

Hermione herself is a surprise to Garnett. His initial impressions of her were as a projection, her "vague personality was merely tributary to her parents," and her "youth and grace were, in some mysterious way, her mother's rather than her own" (595). In fact, so insistent to Garnett is the image of the mother that the daughter's person is utterly "unnoticeable": Hermione is "invisible," a girl "with the smartest woman in London as her guide and example" who had "never developed a taste for dress" and who had "remained simple, unsuspicious and tender, with an inclination to good works and afternoon church" (595). She is in fact, dowdy, and so very different from her mother as to seem to Garnett a changeling, and thus is a symbol for the endless debate of environment versus heredity that Wharton frequently deals with. Hermione is living proof that neither environment nor heredity can determine the outcome of everyone entirely. Until her spectacular match, Hermione is her mother's personal secretary, running errands, writing and answering notes, one of the cogs in the many social wheels Mrs. Newell keeps spinning. Mrs. Newell, essentially, teaches Garnett to see Hermione in this subservient role, and thus he never considers her character.

But Hermione herself astonishes Garnett when she asks him not to contact her father. "Mr. Garnett, he must not be asked – he has been asked too often to do things that he hated...he must not be forced to come unwillingly" (610). Garnett's conversation with her reveals two covert ironies. "'It might be the best thing,' he reflected inwardly'" (610). Garnett's reflection has a double meaning: it might be the best thing for Mr. Newell not to come, thus putting an end to Mrs. Newell's machinations. There is, however, the more covert irony that asking

Garnett to tell Newell not to let himself be used again is the one argument, as Garnett immediately recognizes, that would most likely convince him to be so used. Second, there is the covert irony that Garnett's "heroine" is actually worthy of the name, not just as a victim of her mother's, but in her own right. She represents the moral ideal because she is willing to sacrifice her own personal happiness to preserve her father's hard-won peace. As Garnett recognizes her worthiness his own moral purpose is strengthened. He delivers Hermione's message, and although he knows that the main effect will be to achieve Mrs. Newell's ends, he secretly relishes the covert irony that Mrs. Newell does not see: that Hermione will be "saved" and reunited with her father.

We the audience, therefore, are given the reason not to question Garnett's complicity in undermining the daughter for the sake of the mother; we too buy into the covert righteousness of the action, the inherent morality and goodness that will be its ultimate result. Thus all of the characters, save Garnett, and perhaps Mr. Newell himself, might by types in a kind of social morality play, the scheming mother, the martyred, morally admirable daughter, in which the sins of the former punished by the ultimate salvation of the latter. Mr. Newell's character is troubling, however. Why has he consented to absent himself from his daughter's life? With him, Wharton broaches the problem of filial relationships. Why has Hermione never tried to establish contact? She admits to Garnett that she was not a "child when he left us . . . I was old enough to see" (610). Her plea that he should be left alone and in peace is telling. She accepts her own culpability in the disintegration of this relationship, and "confesses" this via the message Garnett delivers to Mr. Newell. That Mr. Newell himself does not allow her to sacrifice her future happiness for his peace washes him somewhat free, in Garnett's eyes, of the responsibility of leaving her under the negative influences of his wife, thus allowing Garnett to wax sentimental: "in the first flush of his success Garnett had pictured himself as bringing about the father and daughter, and hovering in an attitude of benediction over a family group in which Mrs.

Newell did not very distinctly figure" (612).

But Mrs. Newell does figure. Thus the story ends with the juxtaposition of these two ends: Garnett's revelation of Mrs. Newell's masterpiece, the marriage that "seal[s] and symbolize[s] her social rehabilitation," and Garnett's own moral justification that he has brought together an estranged father and daughter, whose separation was caused by Mrs. Newell. Those morally in the right are saved, but with respect to the reflector himself, all he succeeds in doing is to give way to the need to be morally upright. Garnet recognizes that he has been exploited, but what is covertly ironic is that he does not see his own exploitation of the situation, and the distant involvement in it to secure his own rectitude.

Indeed, Garnett notes that initially he wanted no part of the world of the Newells, but that the position of "London correspondent" to the "New York *Searchlight* required him to interview such people. However, as much as he wants the critical distance his job and purpose give him, such interviews give him a direct view of a world in which he would like to participate: "the great world caldron of art, politics and pleasure – of that high-spiced brew which is nowhere else so subtly and variously compounded – had bread in him an eagerness to taste of the heady mixture" (594). He sees himself as superior, detached, from the Mrs. Newells of the world, and yet he secretly wants to be identified with them; he must find ways, unconsciously, to maintain that superiority and distance from the superficial glitter that so attracts him. There is, then, much personal moral ambiguity, ironically, in Garnett's ending note of smug satisfaction in having done something good in spite of Mrs. Newell's bad.

Furthermore, through Garnett, Wharton addresses a double standard that she also deals with in *The House of Mirth* and *The Custom of the Country*. While a man's earning money and living modestly might not affect his social standing, this is not true for a woman, whose social status would most definitely decline if she were to work; she would "come down in the world." Certainly no young woman of Wharton's own social set would have been allowed, much less have desired, employment, let alone economic self-sufficiency such as Wharton's own. Wharton does not therefore represent herself through her spectator Garnett, but rather, uses him to criticize what is wrong with society. Mrs. Newell ultimately lacks the options available to the financially self-supporting Garnett, who may both work and be accepted into society. Wharton ultimately is just as critical of this double standard that Garnett represents as she is of Mrs. Newell and her incessant social climbing.

Unlike "The Other Two" and "The Last Asset," Wharton's story "The Long Run" is the only story in this chapter to have as its ostensible reflector narrator a first- person narrator, rather than third person limited narration. This unnamed narrator serves to frame the story, providing the true reflector, Halston Merrick, the occasion for which he may reveal his story. This narrator acts as Merrick's "confidant, confessor, and interpreter," and is Merrick's true reflector, allowing Merrick to see what he has become in the long run (Nettels 250-251). And almost immediately, our view of Merrick is shaped by this first-person narrator's biased assessment of him: Merrick has come down in the world. Having made a brilliant start at Harvard, his post-university life, it seems to our frame narrator, is disappointing. Merrick never sells the family business he has inherited and our narrator "was among those disposed to regret Merrick's drop to the level of the prosperous" (Wharton 302). He continues, "there was something more fundamental the matter with Merrick, something dreadful; unforeseen, unaccountable: Merrick had grown conventional and dull"— but dull by whose standards? (303). What qualifies this narrator, of whom we know nothing except that he has been away from New York for over a decade, to pass such judgment on his old friend? Like Garnett and Waythorn, this narrator sees himself as elite, distinct from the ordinary, and above the mere concerns of money. He is an intellectual who sees himself as separate from the consumerist culture surrounding him, and clearly there was a time when Merrick too was a member of this club. But he has changed; the frame narrator laments Merrick's sinking to the level of the common:

> the worst of it was that Merrick – Merrick, who had once felt
> everything! – didn't seem to feel the lack of spontaneity in my
> remarks, but hung on them with a harrowing faith in the
> resuscitating power of our past. It was as if he hugged the empty
> vessel of our friendship without perceiving that the last drop of its
> essence was dry. (303)

But even as the frame narrator admits to his own tendency to hyperbolize, he catalogues Merrick's physical merits, which are still impressive, despite his awkward conversation. In an important essay, "Gender and First Person Narration In Edith Wharton's Short Fiction," Elsa Nettels mentions that the narrator of this story is typical: his role is to divulge information about the characters central to the action of the stories (250). He sometimes takes part in this action, but he is more often non-participatory; he is usually an unmarried intellectual and typically he is financially autonomous, granting him sufficient time to pursue his chosen intellectual activity (247). Such narrators see themselves as superior to those around them, except for other men with similar status, who form a "brotherhood" whose membership they relish (247). In fact, Nettels argues, such narrators represent Wharton's fictionalizing of many of her friends and mentors: the Walter Berrys, Howard Sturgises, Henry Jameses (248). But why does Wharton not model her narrators after Vernon Lee? The few female narrators there are in her short fiction tend to be bright, but they lack Wharton's own "social authority" as well as her social status (257). Nettels suggests that the reason Wharton uses a male narrator so much more often has to do with her general "preference" for male, rather than female company (248-249). It is also related to the predominating view that literature is a "male arena." After all, Goethe, Schiller, Balzac, and Tolstoy, Wharton's primary literary role models, are all male (248-249). Although Wharton did not endow female narrators with her own knowledge of art, literature or science, the female narrators seem to be more intuitive, whereas the male narrators tend to be "blind to the meaning of their own behavior" and "misjudge others," "unwittingly reveal[ing] their own obtuseness and egotism" (251-252). It is the male narrators who are blessed with literary fluency and "rhetorical effect" (257). They are the storytellers and interpreters in Wharton's fiction, and despite the more "insightful" comments of female narrators it is the male narrators whom Wharton gives the power of allusion. Nettels correctly concludes that Wharton uses men to tell women's stories to "foreshadow the modern scholar's recovery of forgotten women's texts," and challenging the typical gender problems of the early twentieth century (257-258). In "The Long Run," Wharton gives a voice to a woman who, as she states in the story's subtitle, is one of " 'those . . . that had no tongue'" (Wharton 301).

Merrick, our reflector narrator, tells Paulina Trant Reardon's story while reflecting on his own thoughts as well (Nettels 252). Wharton generates irony with these kinds of narrators, and particularly with this conversation between Merrick and the unnamed frame narrator, from the ambiguous gap between what these men can understand about the women's lives they reveal, and what within them inhibits this understanding. We can only hear third hand the buried story of Paulina Trant Reardon, a woman who begins like Wharton herself, with self-authority, at ease in a man's world. Paulina, when Merrick first meets her, seems to be endowed with all that one would like but never find in most of Wharton's female narrators. That this story is not told in her first-person voice, as we shall see, is significant.

When we first meet Paulina, we see her as we see Merrick, through the eyes of the frame narrator, who fails at first to even recognize her. He immediately discounts her as worn, unfashionable, with "a small unvarying smile which might have been pinned on with her ornaments" (Wharton 303). He assumes her to be the same as those surrounding her, one of the denizens of Old New York, who are conventional, dull, having the "obsolete quality" of "nice[ness]" (304). Paulina, before Merrick's revealing narrative, looks to our frame narrator to be "soft but blurred, like the figures in that tapestry behind her" (305). The frame narrator sees Merrick in much the same way, and Merrick recognizes this, commenting that "she struck you like that stuff I gave you to read last night. She's conformed -- I've conformed -- the mills have caught us and ground us: ground us, oh, exceedingly small" (307). Paulina has lost her earlier "rarity," and only Merrick, in explaining his own losses, can explain hers.

Merrick, typical of Wharton's best male narrators, ironically recovers his lost poetic eloquence when recalling the first time he saw Paulina in the same place that the two men rediscover her so changed:

> For the first time I saw a meaning in the stale phrase of a picture's walking out of a frame. For, after all, most people *are* just that to us: pictures, furniture, the inanimate accessories of our little island areas of sensation. And then sometimes one of these graven images moves and throws out live filaments toward us, and the line they make draws us across the world as the moon track seems to draw a boat across the water. (308)

Indeed, Merrick alludes to a romantic Whitmanian Transcendentalism – " It brought forth filament, filament, filament out of itself,' as Whitman himself states in "A Noiseless, Patient Spider," discussing the instantaneous connections or correspondences one might make with another.[1] Merrick waxes transcendental yet again: "the whole of life was in us two, flowing back and forth between us" (309). Yet despite the "emotional currents" he feels between them, he remains merely her friend, until Trant, the "gray" "wooden escort," of a first husband, plans to leave New York and to take her with him (309-310). Merrick speaks accurately about a wife's plight early in the century: "She was Trant's and not mine: part of his luggage when he traveled as she was part of his household furniture when he stayed at home" (311). Merrick shows rare insight here; speaking un-ironically, he is surprisingly perceptive in recognizing the habitual objectifying of women. He also does this earlier in his narrative, when he

---

[1] Whitman, Walt. "A Noiseless Patient Spider" *Leaves of Grass* 1868

comments on how Paulina could have married Trant in the first place. "Queer how we sneer at women for wanting the thing that gives them half their attraction," namely a little "enjoyment," and "a little luxury" – poverty is rarely attractive (309). That Paulina rises above this, and above her husband's small-minded, parochial "prejudices and . . . principles" reveals her independent, non-conforming spirit: "from the first, Paulina had never made the least attempt to change her tone or subdue her colors ...she smoked, she talked subversively, she did as she liked and went where she chose" (309-310). In fact, she lived like a man, moving about the world with a male sense of freedom and self-authority, refusing to let her husband's "stiff frock-coated and tall-hatted mind" force her to conform to his own or any conventional sense of the world, any "shadowy moral etiquette" (310). Merrick also admires Paulina for being an unsentimental realist who "look[s] at facts as they are, without any throwing of sentimental limelights. She knew Trant could no more help being Trant than she could help being herself" (310). Paulina recognizes how the pressures of Old New York culture could create a Philip Trant, proving her to be an accurate interpreter or reader of culture.

Paulina understands that the impending trip will force the issue of the friendship between her and Merrick as well. And again, in his relating to our narrator the agony of deciding their future, he recollects in a Whitmanian way an afternoon in the country, recalling a feeling of connectedness with her and with the world which, for the moment, overrides his "sensation...that she seemed part of life's huge league against him" (312). For Merrick is the type of man who has a sense of destiny, a sense that he was meant for something more than the menial "Works" which he had failed to sell and meant to share that something more with Paulina. Even though she is female, if she accepts his view and rejects convention by rejecting Trant, Paulina is on Merrick's side, one of the "brotherhood" in which Merrick and the frame narrator enjoy membership. If she rejects Merrick, however, she is "part of life's huge league" against him, "more conventional, less genuine" than he had originally thought (312). Merrick not only values her "genuineness" and uncoventionality, he needs it, for it, ironically, validates his own. He sees himself in her; without her he cannot be the man he wants to be, a man of "heightened emotion" and perception who needs the financial freedom to "get away, to see new places and rub up against different ideas" (308).

But this perception of himself is false; ironically, it is she and not he who is genuinely unconventional when she arrives in Riverdale and asks him to send for her trunk: "'I haven't come for a night; if you want me I've come for always'" (314). She is willing to leave her husband for him, but instead of embracing and accepting her, he pulls back. He reflects, "I had supposed her, for all her freedom and originality, to be as tacitly subservient to that view as I was: ready to take what she wanted on the terms on which society concedes such taking, and to pay for it by the usual restrictions, concealments and hypocrisies" (315). In other words, Merrick expected her to cross the "border" from friendship into passion and become his lover, " 'play[ing] the game'" by keeping their affair hidden (311, 315). He never expected that she would go to the extreme she does. She sees the irony of his inconsistency before he does: "'Why you'll take a night and not a life?'" (315).

But her remark to him is just a quip. She, however, realizes that while she herself is genuinely unconventional, he is not. Paulina is willing to put the authenticity of her feelings for Merrick before the dubious morality of a society that dictates hypocritically that, on the one hand, she may have those feelings, but on the other, that she must conceal them. She may not validate them by leaving a man for whom she has no feelings. " 'This thing between us isn't an ordinary thing...and when two people feel that about each other they must live together – or part...it's the high seas – or else being tied up to Lethe Warf. And I'm for the high seas, my dear!'" (316). Wharton herself subscribes to Paulina's viewpoint, commenting to Charles DuBois, "'Ah the poverty, the miserable poverty, of any love that lies outside of marriage, of any love that is not a living together, a sharing of all!'" (qtd. in White 159). Though written earlier than this comment, "The Long Run," like "The Reckoning" and "Souls Belated," struggles with the distinction society makes between love and marriage, and the consequences when the two do not coincide. By telling Paulina's story Wharton challenges not only society's conventional notions of marriage, but the meaning of conventionality itself: is Paulina more or less conventional when she concedes to Merrick's wishes to keep their affair on conventional terms? She puts society itself to the test, to see what results in the long run of their unfulfilled relationship. Wharton's morality with respect to marriage is "contextual" – she provides alternatives in her stories, here the opposite alternative to that presented in "Souls Belated," without choosing either one ultimately as the better. But while in many of Wharton's stories divorce is not the best solution, it is for Paulina within the context of this story and this set of circumstances (White 79-80). For Merrick is as pedantic, "frock-coated and tall-hatted," as Trant himself. One may ignore one's upbringing, Wharton suggests, but one may never escape it. Thus Merrick is concerned only about taking care of Paulina in her "helplessness," "think[ing] for" her, and objectifying her just as Trant does, despite his earlier moments of elucidation. The irony rests in his questioning of her genuineness and conventionality, when he himself is utterly conventional (Brown 71).

Paulina argues poignantly for her position, eloquently positing the difficulties of loving and living this way:

> "first working as a fever in the blood distorting and deflecting
> everything, making all other interests insipid, all other duties
> irksome, and then, as the acknowledged claims of life regained
> their hold, gradually dying – the poor starved passion! – for want
> of the wholesome necessary food of common livings and doings,
> yet leaving life impoverished by the loss of all it might have been."
> (317)

She speaks, not theoretically, but rather contextually – of "'you and me.'" Unlike Julia Westall, Paulina refuses to create a theory or doctrine to justify her relationships – rather, she concerns herself with the possibilities of this one relationship and not "the general rule" that Merrick cannot release (317).

Paulina further argues that Merrick had previously claimed to want to live a 'real' life away from society, "thinking rather than doing" (318). But just as Merrick is unable to do without society's approbation of a relationship, he is unable to do without society itself. Not "being called on" secretly appalls him (318). And even though, at the time, he recognizes that he is not acting as a "novel hero" would by accepting her courageous offer, he could not overcome the notion that "the demon of illusion spoke through her lips," and that she failed to see the consequences of her actions as clearly as he could. She cries for authenticity, for him to validate her real self: " 'Now I have to think of all the tedious trivial trifles I can pack the days with, because I'm afraid – I'm afraid – to hear the voice of the real me, down below, in the windowless hole where I keep her'" (319).

But when he refuses to listen, failing to respond to the utmost cries of the soul to which he professes such an elemental connection, she challenges his counter-arguments that she is not considering the consequences, proposing, " 'No: there's one other way…and that is, *not* to do it! To abstain and refrain; and then see what we become, or what we don't become, in the long run'" (319). But even this challenge cannot move him. Just as he did earlier, Merrick doubts her "genuineness," and now he doubts her "perfect moral honesty" as well (320). "Her rashness and her beauty" would give her the edge to win him over. "I was once more the creature of all the conventional scruples: I was repeating, before the looking glass of my self-consciousness, all the stereotyped gestures of the "'man of honor'" (320). Pathetically, Merrick is able to see the irony of his response only in retrospect. He is "the dupe of" his "phrase," but at the crucial time he could not recognize this. Merrick generates irony in a way that Waythorn and Garnett cannot, by reflecting ironically on his own "reflecting mind" (321).

When conformity "possessed him," art and the creative process itself fled. Merrick turns to the "Works," previously rejected as beneath him, and submerges himself as a justification of his rejection of Paulina, embracing "such moral compensation" that spouting social truths would allow, and "accept [ing] the old delusion that the social and the individual man are two" (321). But Merrick ultimately realizes the futility of this delusion: "in rejecting what had seemed to me a negation of action I had made all my action negative" (322). By becoming the hero of a moral tale, rather than the romantic lover in a sentimental tale, he "'saved" a weak woman from herself," saved her from "scandal and the misery of self reproach" (323). And later Trant is killed. To the fate-trusting Merrick, his initial rejection seems justifiable. Now he could marry Paulina with the full knowledge and approbation of society. But like Newland Archer in *The Age of Innocence,* Merrick visits her home and leaves without seeing her: "there, between us, was the memory of the gesture I hadn't made, forever parodying the one I was attempting" (323). This reflector ultimately sees the value of the road not taken, but, as Paulina correctly prophesies, he only sees this because they have not taken it. She was right in pleading that "her life: that was the thing at stake!" But when Merrick comments that "a woman's life is inextricably part of the man's she cares for," he ironically fails to consider that, in fact, the reverse is also true. Like Julia Westall, Merrick learns, too late, the value of a loving, reciprocating relationship, whether condoned by society or not. The effect of Wharton's dual narration is that the frame narrator distances us from Merrick, and keeps us from being biased by his perspective. Thus we recognize early on the truth of this covert irony, when Merrick, burdened with a patriarchal society's viewpoints, cannot, even though he is objective enough to be critical of them.

Ultimately, Merrick sees the futility of what has become of them both in the long run, but the ambivalence created by the framing first-person narrator still remains. The frame narrator represents all of the prejudices and biases of the single, intellectual bachelor who feels himself better off for having avoided such entanglements as Merrick's, who wants to know about such things only through a story because they, like Paulina "interest" his curiosity without involving him emotionally (305). Many critics see the ambivalent conclusion – or lack of one – on the marriage question as negative. Barbara White concludes that "for Edith Wharton, if the individual is offered any real choice in life, it is usually a choice between modes of defeat" (160). D.B. Flynn sees the story as one about self-sacrifice and "resignation" (107). M.M. Brown reads the tale as an "echo" of Wharton's own life – it "states, as decisively as Wharton ever states it, her sadness for meaningless convention, her regret that personal life is so often controlled by respectability" (7). But the ambivalent fact that Merrick, for all of his admitted moral self-righteousness may have been right, remains. Wharton explores this ambiguity further in the novels *The Age of Innocence* and in *Ethan Frome*. The latter novel ends in disaster when Ethan and Mattie take the ultimate risk to be together. The former ends with the mitigating happiness of children from an essentially loveless marriage. Wharton never solves the problem of what happens when marriage and love are distinct. The covert unstable irony in this story is that the experiment of doing nothing to solve it as a solution is no solution. Ultimately, Paulina is wrong; she and Merrick both are unhappy, conventional, and utterly diminished by the society that he argues they must bow to – but are they better off? In Wharton's fiction, this question is ongoing. The story validates Wharton's right to ask it, in a society that would not.

"The Temperate Zone," from *Here and Beyond* (1926), returns us to a third person reflector, Willis French. He is the ironic reflector par excellence, since we do not actually meet the real Donald Pauls until the very end of the story. Using French generates heaps of ironies since we receive our knowledge of them entirely through his vascillating consciousness that both idolizes and condemns them. The story of the real Pauls only unfolds between these two poles of disenchantment and deification.

From the very start French admits his tongue-in-cheek stance towards the world. "And now, by a turn or what he fondly called his luck – as if no one else's had ever been quite as rare – he found his vacation prolonged, and his prospect of enjoyment increased, by the failure to meet the lady in London" (Wharton 450). French is a character whose own view, initially, is ironic; he resembles Waythorn in being able to laugh at absurd situations, including his own: "Willis French had more than once had occasion to remark that he owed some of his luckiest moments to his failures. He had tried his hand at several of the arts, only to find, in each case, the same impassable gulf between vision and execution; but his ill success, which he always promptly recognized, had left him leisure to note and enjoy all the incidental compensations of the attempt" (450). French is a realist, able to turn the ironic lens inward to evaluate his own successes and failures both sincerely and amusedly, suggesting a maturity lacking in more self-blind figures such as Garnett, who is consumed by the need to do something morally in the right. French's mentors Horace Fingall, the painter, and Emily Morland, the poet, had impressed upon him the paradoxical point that he lives by: "interesting failures may be worth more in the end than dull successes" (450).

But while French can objectively apply this dictum to his own artistic attempts, he, like Paulina Anson, is "a pilgrim to the shrine of genius" (452). He dwells on "his two great initiators," different in every way except for one: "the effect they produced of the divine emanation of genius" (451). Knowing all aspects of this genius is paramount to French. He sees, therefore, no irony at all in the coincidence of his publisher requesting a book on Fingall's art, nor does he see it in the coincidence of Fingall's widow marrying Morland's former fiancée. "Here was an occasion to obtain the desired light, and to obtain it, at one stroke, through the woman who had been the preponderating influence in Fingall's art, and the man for whom Emily Morland had written her greatest poems" (451). What high hopes French has pinned on the Donald Pauls! Thus he is quite cheerful to chase them back to Paris, having failed to see them in London, for he is certain that they are the repositories of their respective lovers' genius, the "custodians of great memories," founts of useful information about their greatness. Wharton here, as in "The Angel at the Grave," uses religious language to emphasize the underlying irony. French is willing to worship gods who are only deities by association, clearly indicating to us with only a degree of covertness that the Pauls are ultimately likely to topple from their lofty heights. Even the sacred home of the poet herself is not "too sacred for the feet of Horace Fingall's widow" (452). That Mrs. Paul herself would think to "desecrate" it by renting or selling it never occurred to him, but this first instance of disillusionment with his gods does not shake French's ardor. When taken for a prospective buyer, French the realist seizes the moment; though "his disenchantment rose to his lips" and "though the mere thought of hiring was a desecration" he gladly enters the previously unseen inner sanctum, illusions intact (452).

It is, therefore, more covertly ironic that French, seeing the inner shrine himself, is glad that it has not been preserved as Morland's "Historic House," such as Orestes Anson's has. French is more utilitarian: he likes "the unknown Donald Pauls the better for living naturally in this house which had come to them naturally, and not shrinking into the mere keepers of a shrine" (453). How paradoxically ironic that French could at once be utterly opportunist, and at the same time be sanguine, for what should have added to his disenchantment with the Pauls only seems to lift them even higher in his estimation. Thus, neither the pink toilet table in Mrs. Morland's dressing room, nor the library being reassigned to Paul bother him in the least.

But what does bother him immensely is Mrs. Paul's portrait hanging over Emily Morland's writing table. "Its presence there shook down all manner of French's faiths. There was something shockingly crude in the way it made the woman in possession triumph over the woman who was gone" (454). For the second time, French's ideals are shaken, and Mrs. Paul threatens to fall from her pedestal. Her beautiful face on the wall of the plain but passionate poet, who died before finding happiness with the man whom her successor married rankles French. But even this "sense of injustice" is not one he can sustain for long.

Ironically, despite himself "the thought of Mrs. Morland was displaced by the vision of her successor," as he departs for France to meet his idol in person (455).

But what are the Pauls "really like" (456)? French's image of them is hazy at best. He only gleans information about their past by hearsay. She is a remade woman of poor social background, like an Undine Spragg or an Alice Waythorn, while he comes from a good family but was "a not especially rising young barrister" with nothing much but his looks to recommend him (456). While French creates his own image of his gods, he continues to be utterly un-ironic. The "omissions" in Lady Branklehurst's information, he thinks, reveal "something too fine and imponderable" about them," and nothing that Lady Brankelhurst imparts about them, despite their "crude" beginnings, can tarnish their gleam in French's mind (456).

But French's mind is quick to return to its ironic perspective when directed towards something other than his beloved Pauls. The young elegant couple that the portraitist Jolyesse points out piques French's momentary interest. To the painter, the couple is all one could hope for in future models. To French, however, their studied elegance is "stale," and the woman in particular "had the air of wearing her features, like her clothes, simply because they were the latest fashion, and not because they were a part of her being" (459, 458). So fixed is his idea that the Pauls must look noble on the outside to reflect their inner noble state as the vessels of greatness that French feels himself quite adept at gauging the inner emotional state of others simply by pondering their exteriors. "Her inner state was probably a much less complicated affair than her lovely exterior: it was a state, French guessed, of easy apathetic good humor, galvanized by the occasional need of a cigarette, and by a gentle enjoyment of her companion's conversation" (459). This is covertly ironic, because it is French's very un-ironic vision of the Pauls that creates the basis of comparison between them and the almost instantaneously ironic perception of the couple before him.

Fingall's still-living rival Jolyesse provides the subtext of the story, a discussion of art and taste. Jolyesse shrewdly comments to French that perhaps Fingall was not really so great an artist:

> "Of course he sells *now* -- tremendously high, I believe. But that's what happens; when an unsuccessful man dies, the dealers seize on him and make him a factitious reputation. Only it doesn't last. You'd better make haste to finish your book; that sort of celebrity collapses like a soap bubble. . . .Fingall had aptitudes -- immense, no doubt -- but no technique, and no sense of beauty; none whatever." (458)

His quips are not merely an astute commentary on Fingall's debatable artistic merit, but also on the commercializing and commodifying of artistic worth in general. Fingall was not, according to Jolyesse, a great artist, but yet posthumously, he sells like one – public taste is undiscriminating. If something sells, then it must be valuable; it has no worth until a price tag has been attached. French is far too honest and too intelligent not to recognize his own self-interest, as he also considers public taste.

> Intolerable as it was to French to think that snobbishness and cupidity were the chief elements in the general acclamation of his idol, he could not forget that he owed to these baser ingredients the chance to utter his own panegyric. It was because the vulgar herd at last wanted to know what to say, when it heard Fingall mentioned, that Willis French was to be allowed to tell them; such was the base rubble the Temple of Fame was built of!" (459)

French's thesis is that the private and artistic lives of the artist are inextricably intertwined. What French does not want to admit is that the value of the art that has been produced, whatever the source, is not something intrinsically determinable, but is only subject to the "cupidity" of the paying audience; artistic value is only measurable in consumerist terms. This contributed, perhaps, to Fingall's failure as an artist during his own lifetime. For, as Mrs. Paul points out, he "'painted only for himself'" and "'simply despised popularity'" (461). Art for art's sake, Wharton clearly implies here, might be a worthy ideal, but not realistic in a world that looks first at the reputation of the artist, and at the cost of the piece. Mrs. Paul, when she finally does speak, uses words that, to French, could have "no meaning for her save, as it were, a symbolic one; they were like the mysterious price marks with which dealers label their treasures" (461). Mrs. Paul, French learns, is the ultimate representative of the consumerist culture her husband despised. She comments that the posthumous recognition that Fingall has been receiving, " 'the kind of recognition even *he* would have cared for,'" is not that of the serious art world, but once again that of a greedy public eager to own: " 'the dealers are simply fighting for his things'" (461-462). It is, French notes, "the only measure of greatness she knew . . . in any art, the proof and corollary of greatness was to become a best seller" (462).

Thus French revises his vision of her simultaneously with his understanding of her sense of Fingall's greatness. No longer an enigma, she is superficial, a "too-smiling beauty set in glasses and glitter, preoccupied with dressmakers and theater stalls," who wounds French deeply by trivializing his mentor's greatness by "affirming her husband's genius in terms of the auction room and the stock exchange" (462). French's own creative endeavor is in jeopardy, but he pins his hopes on Mr. Paul, whose relationship with the great poet "must have given him a sense of values more applicable than Mrs. Paul's to French's purpose" (463).

But Mr. Paul is hardly more promising an emissary of his former love's greatness than is his wife, shocking French when, on a visit to Fingall's studio, Paul fails to recognize the sketch of Emily Morland "aquiver in every line with life and sound and color" that French discovers in a sketchbook he finds (467). Showing as little artistic discrimination as his wife, Paul is amazed that French "like[s] this sort of thing," and is happy, even relieved, to turn over the writing of Morland's "life" to French (469). But French's last ideal is shattered when Mrs. Paul later reminds him that he will be taking on the writing of the biography "in return for the precious thing he's given you" (470). To French's horror, he finally learns the truth about his idols: they are utterly the creatures of the consumerism surrounding them. "After all," Mrs. Paul claims, "business is business, isn't it?"

French learns the hard way that the Pauls are, as both Mr. and Mrs. Paul are quick to point out, "ordinary mortals, who don't live among the gods" and "can't afford to give nothing for nothing" (471). Miserably French compares this to his vision of Fingall himself, who

> must have lived so intensely and constantly in his own inner vision that nothing external mattered. He must have been almost as detached from the visible world as a great musician or a great ascetic; at least till ones at him down before a face or a landscape—and then what he looked at became the whole of the visible world to him. (466)

French's first instinct is to "get away at any cost" (470). However, the story ends with Mrs. Paul thrilled that in exchange for his doing the Fingall book, French will arrange for Jolyesse, the rival painter whom Mrs. Paul really admires, to do her portrait at a discount. This ending itself is unambiguous, but what is ambiguous and therefore ironically covert and unstable is the conclusion French draws about artistic worth in a consumerist society. Does he merely give in to the overwhelming commercial force that the Pauls represent? Or is French the same opportunist he was before his grand illusions are shattered, preserving his ideals of artistic greatness, while using any means to glean the information he needs to achieve his own creative ends? And to what extent does that compromise his artistic integrity? Wharton's ironic reflector does not reveal the answers to these questions. As in "The Long Run," the reflector's purpose is not to provide answers, but to provide the occasion for these important questions to be asked.

Chapter Three
Self-Conscious, Self-Ironized

In Chapter Two we examined Wharton's use of a reflecting spectator narrator to tell the story. In that group of stories, Wharton's narrator, sometimes first-person, generates irony through his own ironic perspective of the events he narrates, or from his own complicit participation in those events, despite the self-proclaimed role of "spectator." These ironies are covert and stable but are not local, because the stories end in ambiguity, without a clear resolution of the ironic situation at hand.

In Chapter three, we will examine how Wharton relies entirely on third-person narration to create irony, by suppressing or omitting an observer or spectator narrator altogether. Wharton generates irony vis-à-vis the central reflecting consciousness of the protagonists in this group of stories. We have no omniscient editorial voice offering sarcastic quips, nor do we have an urbane spectator on the fringe of the action offering an ironic commentary. Rather, Wharton establishes a close relationship between her central characters and us, the audience, without interference by an intermediary. She creates and undermines covert, infinite ironies in the gap between what the audience knows or understands about a fictive situation within a story, and the "psychological reality" of what the central character knows or understands. This character's comprehension of his or her own limitations, or, as the case may be, lack of comprehension, also generates fragile ironies. Is a character more ironic for having some understanding of his or her situation, though unable to effect a change, or less so? Or, are the characters who are most unaware the most ironic of all?

Little treated by scholars, "The Muse's Tragedy," first published in *Scribner's Magazine* in January of 1899, is one such story about which we might pose the above question. It provides us with two central characters, and therefore at least two versions of what can happen when delusion or misinterpretation clouds one from seeing things as they really are.

The story begins as Danyers' story, the story of how this literary critic meets the muse of his literary idol, Vincent Rendle. Danyers, initially, is another male version of Paulina Anson: a worshipper whose devotion is centered on his hero's intellectual success, rather than on the personality and personal life of the figure himself. With this distinction, Wharton again calls into question the nature of art and aesthetic value. Mrs. Memorall represents the reading public: "the kind of woman," Danyers thinks, "who runs cheap excursions to celebrities" (Wharton 68). Mrs. Memorall only engages Danyers's interest when she begins to speak of her old school chum Mary Anerton, Rendle's muse. But the type of information she is able to impart has more to do with Rendle's personal habits than with his literary ones. "Rendle," she tells us, "always had to have a certain seat at the dinner table, away from the draft and not too near the fire, and a box of cigars that no one else was allowed to touch" (69). Mrs. Memorall quips sarcastically about Rendle's fussiness, yet offers no more of what Danyers would deem intellectual substance, only "rude[ly] fingering" Danyers' "idol" (69). Wharton, through Danyers, reflects ironically upon Mrs. Memorall's taste and her tendency to popularize a literary figure, turning him into a celebrity. "She was like a volume of unindexed and discursive memoirs, through which he patiently plodded in the hope of finding embedded amid layers of dusty twaddle some precious allusion to the subject of his thought" (70). Here, as in "The Angel at the Grave," Wharton cloaks Danyers' admiration of the poet Rendle in religious language throughout the first part of the story, thereby distinguishing between the "sacredness" of true literary taste and critical judgment, and the more gauche interests of popular culture. Danyers "worship[s]" Rendle for his "divine" and "immortal" verse (68). Mrs. Memorall's "careless familiarity with the habits of his divinity" annoys him, especially when she sarcastically comments on "Vincent Rendle's way of taking his tea," which "has become a sacred rite" (68). Such an alignment of Rendle's personal habits with that which, in Danyers' eyes, is "sacred" is more than insulting to him – it is sacrilege, and only Mrs. Memorall's fount of information about Mrs. Anerton holds his contempt for the former at bay.

Not surprisingly, Danyers extends this quasi-religious admiration of Rendle to his muse: she is "included in his worship of Rendle" (68). We see the first glimpse of Wharton's covert infinite irony in the story when Danyers' view changes somewhat with personal knowledge of Mary Anerton. Initially, Mrs. Anerton is a Paulina-like handmaiden, preserving Rendle's intellect in trust via her own:

> Of the master's intellectual life, of his habits of thought and work, she never wearied of talking. She knew the history of each poem; by what scene or episode each image had been evoked; how many times the words in a certain line had been transposed; how long a certain adjective had been sought, and what had at last suggested it; she could even explain that one impenetrable line, the torment of critics, the joy of detractors, the last line of *The Old Odysseus*. (72)

But unlike Paulina, who can only know her god second hand through the works he has bequeathed to her guardianship, Mrs. Anerton knew the man himself. Thus can Mrs. Anerton satisfy every one of Danyers' bursts of intellectual curiosity; she does not merely "echo" Rendle's thoughts, parroting them as Paulina Anson might have done (72). Rather, Mary Anerton is the keeper of hitherto "impenetrable" mysteries – she is "the custodian of Rendle's inner self, the door, as it were, to the sanctuary" that the acolyte Danyers so wishes to enter (72). We see the first covert irony when Danyers, prepared to pray at what he believed to be her lesser altar, becomes willing to worship her in her own right, seeing himself as "one more grain of frankincense on the altar of her insatiable divinity" (71).

Interestingly, Wharton creates a covertly ironic reversal by using her male character in the story, rather than her female ones, to suggest that women have value as the source of, and not merely as the object of, artistic production: "If her identity had appeared to be merged in his [Rendle's] it was because they thought alike, not because he thought for her ….Danyers began to see how many threads of his complex mental tissue the poet had owed to the blending of her temperament with his"; Danyers, crediting Mary Anerton with a unique mind and temperament, sees women as more than the "chance pegs on which" poets have "hung their garlands" (72). They are a possible source or origin of art, organic, not merely mimetic: Mrs. Anerton is the "fertile garden" within which Rendle's roots can grow and flower (72). But undermining the initial irony of Danyers' opinion of Mrs. Anerton is Wharton's interweaving of both praise for and criticism of Mrs. Anerton's role via the ironically reversed, contrasting views of Danyers and Mrs. Memorall. For it is Mrs. Memorall who voices the more conventionally feminist protest of Mary Anerton's seeming hero-worship of Rendle: "…she was always so engrossed, so preoccupied…The fact is, she cared only about his friends -- she separated herself from all her own people" (68-69). According to Mrs. Memorall, then, Mrs. Anerton (not to mention the "ridiculous" Mr. Anerton as well) has allowed her very self identity to be subsumed by Rendle's, even posthumously: "'She misses him too much – her life is too empty'" sighs Mrs. Memorall (69). Represented by Mrs. Memorall's view of Mrs. Anerton, women could be both artistic consumers and muses, but not "artistic observers" (Singley 30). This is why only Danyers can voice the idea of woman as artist. Conventionally only Danyers, as a man, can be the writer. Mrs. Anerton's fate is to be his literary inspiration or, as M. Denise Witzig indicates, the audience of his literary production, thus "inevitably" placing her "outside" or making her "absent from that literary economy, her only profit a further fixing of her position in language and literature" (Witzig 267). As Rendle's muse, Mrs. Anerton is, suggests Cynthia Griffin Wolff, "the perfect, passive incarnation of femininity…a convenient object,'" and as such, has (at least in this section of the story) no true voice of her own (qtd.in Witzig 263). Only Danyers, ironically, is granted the power to speak for her. Is Mary Anerton, then, the ultimate objectified Muse, or is she, as Danyers would have us believe, another Rendle-like "immortal," an artistic creator in her own right? Or is she something else entirely? Wharton's creation of a multiplicity of Mary Anertons spirals us into a constantly shifting kaleidoscope of ironies forever changing hue and focus.

Wharton yet again overturns the fragile irony she has established. For just as we begin to appreciate her male character's more pro-feminist viewpoint of women as potential creators in their own right, Danyers reverts to conventionality, believing, as the two develop a more intimate relationship, that perhaps she could become his own wellspring, his goddess, *his* muse. Mrs. Anerton encourages Danyers, hitherto "so small an actuality," "to speak of himself; to confide his ambitions to her," and tells him to write: "How she had divined him; lifted and disentangled his groping ambitions; laid the awakening touch on his spirit with her creative *Let there be light!*" (Wharton 72-73). Danyers is willing both to worship her as his new god, and to appropriate her for his own potential artistic production. Thus in the first part of the story, the "real" Mary Anerton is absent, merely an idea, "undimensional, featureless, enigmatic; Mary embedded within myth" (Witzig 265).

Even as he falls in love with her, Danyers is unable to see or to know the real Mary, or to read what Witzig calls her "full textual presence" (269). Instead Danyers must intellectualize, aestheticize, and therefore deify both her and his rather ordinary human feelings for her. Wharton again creates irony through the overturning of a convention, here the conventional notion of love as an extraordinary, exalted feeling or state of human existence. The ideal of true love is not what Danyers wants – he wants the embodiment of an intellectual ideal, as he sees her, and it is this with which he falls in love. When Mrs. Anerton suggests to Danyers " 'you ought to write a book about *him*,'" meaning, of course, Rendle, Danyers' immediate jealousy is both personal and intellectual, when he sarcastically notices "Rendle's way of walking in unannounced" (Wharton 73). Danyers wants her to love him in his own right, but he also wants her to be his own conduit to literary greatness, not merely for her to turn him into yet another means of perpetuating Rendle's. By writing "a complete interpretation – a summing up of his style, his purpose, his [Rendle's] theory of life and art," Danyers could, paradoxically, both maintain his personal and intellectual relationship with Mary Anerton and potentially destroy it, as long as Rendle's ghost resides at the very center of their shared lives (73). Thus Wharton ends the first part of this story, leaving Danyers in the covertly ironic state of which old wisdom warns us: be careful what you wish for, for it may come true. Danyers has received what he has wished for, the chance to study his idol unfettered, but not without cost.

In the second part of the story, Mary Anerton's letter to Danyers, ending this tenuous relationship, reads more like a journal, allowing us into her psychological reality to see the truth, as she represents it. M. Denise Witzig argues that Mary Anerton's letter "deconstruct[s] and de[fies] meaning in her absolute appropriation of the production of the text" (269). But perhaps rather than defying meaning, Mrs. Anerton becomes a maker of meaning, and appropriates the role of determinant, both of her relationship with Rendle, who (we later learn) could not love her, and of her relationship with Danyers, who loves her as a source of his future artistic production. Ironically, Mary Anerton has had that which is extraordinary – she has scaled the heights of an intellectual Mount Olympus, as far as the public is concerned. The "ordinary," because human and personal, feelings of love and intimacy that have nothing at all to do with intellect are what Mary Anerton wants, but also what she never seems to be able to elicit from the men in her life. But now we hear her voice, and hear her truth: "It is because Vincent Rendle *didn't love me* that there is no hope for you. I never had what I wanted, and never, never, never will I stoop to wanting anything else" (73). They had, rather, an "intellectual sympathy" upon which Rendle "grew dependent," but that was all: "But all the while, deep down, I knew he had never cared" (74-75). She reveals that she allowed herself to become Sylvia through the "whispers" of a society quick to join the two as lovers (75). The hidden irony she exposes here is that she loved him "not because he was Vincent Rendle, but just because he was himself" (74). In other words, she loves him in the common way of it, while he writes his *Sonnets to Silvia* as "a cosmic philosophy, not a love poem; addresssed to Woman, not to a woman" (75). Yet despite knowing this truth, she conspires with these "elderly peeresses, aspiring hostesses, lovesick girls and struggling authors" triumphant in her "success" in recreating herself as the secret love of Rendle's life, via the letters she submits for publication: "Those letters I myself prepared for publication; that is to say, I copied them out for the editor, and every now and then I put in a line of asterisks to make it appear that something had been left out. You understand? The asterisks were a sham – *there was nothing to leave out*" (75). Hildegarde Hoeller, in a book on Wharton and sentimental fiction, suggests that Mary's letter is a corrective female sentimental voice that counters the "'tasteful' ironic male" voice preceding it (Hoeller 55). Perhaps, though, through both her edition of Rendle's letters and her letter to Danyers Mary seizes control of her own narrative, attempting to free herself from her "prison of inarticulateness" (Waid 178). But she does so through a style of "resistance and omission," using the punctuation of omission: "parentheses and dashes, colons and ellipses…asides, reiterations" (Witzig 266). She also uses this strategy in the letter itself: she implies much by her letter, but says little outright about how much time has elapsed, about their meeting in Venice, about the marriage proposal we assume Danyers has made (265). We even infer, not illogically, that this letter has been sent to and read by Danyers, though we have no proof – we only have the letter itself as our touchstone to reality (267). Mary Anerton is thus the consummate artist, controlling the text and our interpretation of it. And while we (and, we are to assume, Danyers) are reeling from the revelation the letter makes, Wharton uncovers yet another, even more covert irony: that, as the artist, the creator of her own public image, Mary Anerton receives critical acclaim, albeit second hand:

The critics, you may remember, praised the editor for his

> commendable delicacy and good taste (so rare in these days!) in omitting from the correspondence all personal allusions, all those *details intimes* which should be kept sacred from the public gaze. They referred, of course to the asterisks in the letters to Mrs. A. (75)

Is this merely Mary's "delusions of a literary critic," as Hoeller argues (55)? Mary's strategy of inference or absence makes her successful as the "real" Mary Anerton who is Rendle's intellectual companion, and, ironically, she is equally successful as her own opposite, the Mary Anerton who is the beloved, but utterly artificial Sylvia. Mary Anerton the woman, failing to be the muse of the man she loves, is also Mary Anerton the artist, her own muse.

Wharton herself is highly critical of the public that has created Rendle's "love" of Mrs. Anerton, and of the taste of a society so eager to believe in it and therefore reinforce it. We clearly hear Wharton through Mary Anerton as her letter progresses:

> Sentimental girls and dear lads like you turned pink when somebody whispered, 'That was Silvia you were talking to.' Idiots begged for my autograph – publishers urged me to write my reminiscences of him – critics consulted me about the reading of doubtful lines. And I knew that, to all these people, I was the woman Vincent Rendle had loved. (77)

As one of Wharton's very few female characters, Mary voices for Wharton, rather pessimistically, the loneliness as well as the irony of her circumstances – Mary loved Rendle despite, and not because of, his literary greatness. That this love was never returned is her great grief: "The intellectual union counted for nothing now. It had been soul to soul, but never hand in hand, and there were no little things to remember him by" (77). Mary, utterly self-aware of the irony, thus experiments with Danyers, for whom she admittedly has affection. His love shows her that she is not unworthy of being loved: "I knew you cared for me! Yes, at that moment really cared" (78). Yet she reads his potential motives clearly, and even when "certain" of his feelings for her, rejects him, making sure that he can never expropriate her story, and turn her "into a pretty little essay with a margin" (78). It is an infinitely covert irony that we cannot even judge the extent of Danyers' recognition of the irony of his own situation, since his voice in the story is quashed by Mary's letter. She controls our understanding of Danyers' emotional state, as well as his previously discussed proposal. Though we never hear his voice declaring, or even implying his love, she is "certain" of it, since he never once in their month in Venice, "mentioned the book" that was his "ostensible reason for coming" (78). Perhaps this certainty is a self-delusion, the ultimate creative act of a woman whose "tragedy," in its most covertly ironic form, is that she wasn't truly tragic: she never knows nor feels real love from the man she loved – she has only a public fiction of it. Mary's unrequited love lacks the grand scale of human emotion and consequences that a conventional sense of tragedy requires; she as muse and Rendle, as artist, have only the fiction of a grand passion. The reality, however, is much smaller, more local; there are simpler feelings that the woman beneath the muse has never truly felt nor had returned. Perhaps most covertly, her "tragedy" in a modern sense is in being deemed the Muse extraordinaire, and therefore never being allowed to be the ordinary and individual Mary.

That Wharton creates in Mary Anerton a kindred spirit seems obvious. There is her own failed marriage to Teddy, an Anerton-like figure, who is ultimately extraneous to the intellectual center of Wharton's life, into which Henry James or Bernard Berenson were admitted; there is Wharton's unconsummated attachment to Walter Berry, her "'beloved'" (Benstock 405). Perhaps this is why Wharton has Mary Anerton suppress Danyers' narrative. It is the only means by which she can illustrate the infinitely covert, because irresolvable tragedy of her own situation: that art and love fight for supremacy in a truly sensitive consciousness, and that the demands of one can only be met at the sacrifice of the other.

Another tale that touches upon this painful truth is "Souls Belated," from

The Greater Inclination (1899). Harry Thurston Peck, reviewing the collection, calls "Souls Belated" "the longest, the strongest, and the most striking of the stories," an "almost painfully absorbing study of motive: (qtd. In *Contemporary Reviews* 20). What makes this tale so painfully absorbing? Here, as in "the Muse's Tragedy," the audience becomes entirely caught up in Wharton's interesting use of limited narration, which provides us with alternative voices – both that of Gannett, the artist, and of Lydia, his lover, again to unravel the entanglement of artistic production with personal relationships. What makes this tale even greater that "The Muse's Tragedy" is the added dimension of the discussion of marriage and the social mores that govern relationships. The majority of the covert, infinite irony here stems from the way each character unconsciously grapples with the ideology of marriage, and how what society deems acceptable subconsciously influences the opinions and actions of each character, regardless of their overtly unconventional stance on the marriage question that the couple takes at the story's beginning. To what extent does the covert irony increase exponentially when Wharton also forces us to consider the needs of the artist?

The story, as M.M. Brown notes, is a dramatizing of Wharton's general ironic perspective, detailing the paradox that Lydia both needs social conventions, and needs to reject them in order to establish selfhood (Brown 113). Lydia, prior to the opening of the story, flaunts convention, choosing to leave her spouse to be with Gannett without the legality, as well as the social nicety, of divorce and remarriage. This is a circumstance unallowable to Newland Archer and Ellen Olenska in, for example, *The Age of Innocence*, and unthinkable to the upwardly mobile Undine Spragg in *Custom of the Country*, who would rather marry herself out of society's reach altogether, than sully her good name. But here, Lydia flits back and forth between the "light" of ironic self-recognition, and the darkness of delusion. Overtly ironic are the motives Lydia ascribes to her leaving Tillotson, which we experience directly here via the third-person narration. She has, she initially believes, left not only Tillotson, who "had himself embodied all her reasons for leaving him" (Wharton 106). She also leaves behind a microcosm of a parochial society, which "revolved in the same circle of prejudices," whose "doctrines" prescribed life down to the minutest detail of what should be done or talked about in every instance of social life (Wharton 106). Here again, there is a parallel between physical and emotional interiors: "The moral atmosphere of the Tillotson interior was as carefully screened and curtained as the house itself: Mrs. Tillotson senior dreaded ideas as much as a draft in her back" (106). Thus Lydia congratulates herself, at first, for escaping such a stifling society, but at the story's opening, contemplating her present difficulties with Gannett, she realizes the irony of her "supreme deliverance" from Tillotson. "Freedom had released her from Tillotson as that it had given her to Gannett. . . Yet she had not left him till she met Gannett. It was her love for Gannett that had made life with Tillotson so poor and incomplete a business" (106). She sees, now that she and Gannett, confronted by Tillotson's divorce papers, are "sorry to be alone" together on their train journey, that she "had left her husband only to be with Gannett" (107). That is, she recognizes her motives for what they really are – the culmination of love and desire, understandable, but ultimately selfish, nonetheless. She was married and she wanted to be with Gannett, so she leaves Tillotson to be with him. That she also leaves behind the conventional society that is Tillotson's world is really secondary to her "readjustment of focus" from Tillotson to Gannett (107). But it is this latter reason that Lydia holds up to herself most of the time as the "real" reason for leaving him: she has, in escaping Tillotson, escaped a stifling, narrow set of conventions about relationships. So, despite her momentary epiphany, she reverts back to this posture of unconventionality once the divorce papers arrive and she is truly free to marry.

Lydia is covertly ironic as she clings to her "principles" against marriage, even though she rightly recognizes what conventional society will say now that marriage to Gannett is truly an option. "Her husband, in casting her off, had virtually flung her at Gannett: it was thus that the world viewed it. The measure of alacrity with which Gannett would receive her would be the subject of curious speculation over afternoon tea tables and in club corners" (107). Perceptively, Lydia sees the "ironical implication" of marrying Gannett, which would "rehabilitate" her in the eyes of society: she, according to society, has violated its moral strictures, and done wrong (107). Marrying her, he would gain some degree of social approbation for having done the "'decent thing,'" and "'stand'" some " 'damage'" as well, whereas she would always raise "'ladies' eyebrows'" (107). Such a marriage, while placing them back inside the bounds of societal acceptance, because it conforms to social expectation and convention, would, therefore, be, to her mind, "the only real disgrace" (107). Marriage to Gannett would mean allowing societal conventions and dictates of morality to govern her behavior, and not what Lydia believes to be her own internal sense of morality; it is the acceptance, publicly, of the opinion that in leaving her husband, she has done wrong, and that intimate non-marital relationships are too. Thus she idealizes her unconventionality, her "voluntary fellowship" with Gannett, and rejects the "bondage" of a marriage (108).

But, as Dale Flynn argues, it is not only society but Lydia herself who does not approve of the state of their relationship, and she cares, despite herself, what society thinks (51): "She knew what would be said – she had heard it so often of others! The recollection bathed her in misery" (Wharton 107). Flynn correctly calls Lydia a "saboteur"

> in spite of herself. . . by caring what society thinks. On the other hand, if she marries him, she yields to that convention she was trying to escape. Thus her supposed solution to an intolerable marriage has merely subjected her to more labyrinthine conflict. She must make a choice between her freedom to love whom she wishes and her internalized need to fulfill society's expectations. (53-54)

Thus Lydia is trapped between her public rejecting of social norms and her subconscious internalizing of those norms – and what is covertly ironic is that the more she senses this trap, the more she clings to her "theory" about marriage and "conventional morality," refusing to "compromise" her ideals (Wharton 110). Lydia argues passionately for her theory:

> "We neither of us believe in the abstract 'sacredness' of marriage; we both know that no ceremony is needed to consecrate our love for each other . . . And the very fact that, after a decent interval, these same people would come and dine with us – the women who talk about the indissolubility of marriage, and who would let me die in a gutter today because I am 'leading a life of sin' – doesn't that disgust you more than their turning their backs on us now?" (Wharton 110).

Lydia justly eschews the hypocrisy of such women, but this only becomes ironic retrospectively. Initially, when Lydia herself suggests that they stay at the Hotel Bellosguardo, towards which they had been journeying in the first part of the story, it is Gannett who balks: "'the place is full of old cats in caps who gossip with the Chaplain. Shall you like – I mean, it would be different if'" (112). He hints, but cannot say directly, that since the place is filled with Mrs. Tillotsons, in their present unmarried state they would be ignored, if not openly disapproved of. If Lydia and Gannet stay they must either conform by getting married, or shock and therefore be rejected by those who would find their relationship distasteful. Gannet's attitude is realistic, but Lydia's response is idealistic in its non-conformist stance: "'do you suppose I care? It's none of their business . . . they may think what they please'" (112). At this point we can only admire the consistency, as well as the passion with which Lydia refuses to compromise her principles.

However, in part three of the story, we get a closer glimpse of those whose opinions Lydia earlier claims to scorn. Lady Susan Condit is the social determinant of this microcosm of fashionable society, the one at the top of the social ladder whose stamp of approval or disapproval decides one's acceptance into her "little family," or rejection from it (115). That Lydia and Gannett are welcome members, and not ostracized, is, from our initial perspective an overt irony, since we have not yet been informed that the couple is posing as a married one. This becomes even more obviously ironic to us, the audience, when Lydia and Gannett are confronted with the "Lintons," a louder, more vulgar nouveau riche version of themselves. Lady Susan "ignored the Lintons, and her little family . . . followed suit" (115). Yet Lydia barely blushes when Miss Pinsent, another "family" member, asks what Lydia's "husband's" opinion of the Lintons is. Lydia certainly does not rush to enlighten Miss Pinsent about the nature of her relationship with Gannett. Lydia thus rapidly differentiates between her own "principled" unconventionality and the more scandalous behavior of the "Lintons," who "'have taken the most expensive suite . . . and they have champagne with every meal,'" flaunting their money and maintaining the flimsiest of marital disguises, "challenging" their "rejection," and "ignor[ing] their ignorers," "behav[ing] exactly as though the hotel were empty" (115). With an indirectness that is tremendously ironic, the narration hints at, without explicitly stating outright that Lydia and Gannett are merely pretending to be married for admittance to Lady Susan's circle. Lydia and Gannett, unlike the "Lintons," had managed to keep the details of their own behavior private, whereas everyone recognizes the real names of the Lintons, Lord Trevenna and Mrs. Cope, who "had figured in a flamboyant elopement which had thrilled fashionable London some six months earlier" (117). Thus Lydia, one of Lady Susan's cherished ignorers, is most disturbed to be confronted with Mrs. Cope's pleas for help, which at first merely suggest the similarity of their respective marital situations: " 'Now you see how it is – you understand, don't you?'" (117). Even when the moment reaches its crisis, and Mrs. Cope comes as close as she ever will to revealing the truth about Lydia and Gannett in the service of emotional blackmail, she maintains an indirectness of language:

> "Oh, go, by all means – pray don't let me detain you! Shall you go
> and tell Lady Susan Condit that there's a pair of us – or shall I save
> you the trouble of enlightening her . . . You're too good to be
> mixed up in my affairs, are you? Why you little fool, the first day I

laid eyes on you I saw that you and I were both in the same box –
that's the reason I spoke to you." (118)

This pretense of marriage reveals Lydia's unconscious, and therefore hugely covertly ironic, desire to conform, to live according to the very habits and institutions that she outwardly rejects. Lydia lives in one of two states: either constant introspection, or none. Her second epiphany in the story is that she "had lost the habit of introspection" (118). So busy is she conforming to Lady Susan's narrow society and rules of propriety, she has had little time to think, hence again reaching her moment of self realization only through conversation with another – earlier with Gannett, and here with Mrs. Cope. Hugely ironic is that random rumination itself does not produce such self-understanding. Only Mrs. Cope's threat of exposure forces the marriage issue between Gannett and Lydia, which had remained static since their arrival at the Hotel Bellosguardo, to the forefront of their minds once again.

Coupled with the relief Lydia feels at the arrival of Mrs. Cope's divorce papers, obviating the need for Lydia to "spy" on Trevenna, and therefore preserving her secret, is the ironic recognition that she actually does "care" what Lady Susan and her cohorts think. Lydia laughs when Gannett informs her that Lady Susan herself has asked Lydia to be the "'patroness to a charity concert she is getting up'" – something she would enjoy doing (121). Lydia has the pretext of marriage without its protections, and at this point, is able to recognize that she is living the same kind of life abroad with the same kind of people from whom she sought flight. But, again ironically, only conversation, here with Gannett, and not her own inner rumination, provokes the epiphany:

> "I fancied it was for your sake that I insisted on staying . . . But afterwards I wanted to stay myself – I loved it . . . . These people – the very prototypes of the bores you took me away from, with the same fenced-in view of life, the same keep-off-the-grass morality, the same little cautious virtues and the same little frightened vices – well, I've clung to them, I've delighted in them, I've done my best to please them . . . Respectability! It was the one thing in life

> that I was sure I didn't care about, and it's grown so precious to me
> that I've stolen it because I couldn't get it any other way." (123)

What Lydia realizes she wants at this moment, more than anything, is to fit in, to conform: "The one thing that mattered to me...was my standing with Lady Susan'" (122). Lydia, as Dale Flynn puts it, is incapable of "liv[ing] beyond the pale of society," and recognizes this paradox within herself (53).

What makes Lydia nearly intolerable as a character, however, is her continued refusal to modify or compromise her ideals, despite her situation, and despite what she seemingly learns about her own covert conventionality after the incident with Mrs. Cope: "'I, who used to fancy myself unconventional'" (Wharton 122). Of course, Gannett is not only willing to marry her, he wants to, and not merely to restore their respectability, but Lydia refuses.

> "Do you know, I begin to see what marriage is for. It's to keep
> people away from each other. Sometimes I think that two people
> who love each other can be saved from madness only by the things
> that come between them – children, duties, visits, bores, relations
> – the things that protect married people from each other. We've
> been too close together – that has been our sin. We've seen the
> nakedness of each other's souls." (123)

That is, their unconventional love brings them closer together than any conventional marriage would ever allow, and even they, like married couples, need some distance to maintain this relationship. Lydia allows that the institution of marriage, with all of its inherent social and familial obligations, has some value in that it codifies appropriate reasons for having time alone and away from one's beloved. But this epiphany is undermined by denial again; she continues to refuse to compromise, seeing the institution of marriage itself as a deception: "'If I were your wife you'd have to go on pretending. You'd have to pretend that I'd never been – anything else. And our friends would have to pretend that they believed what you pretended'" (123). She emphasizes to Gannett the fiction within a fiction: "'it's our being together that's impossible. I only want you to see that marriage won't help it'" (123). Leaving him is the only option that Lydia sees;

she rationalizes that "'it's because I care –'" (124). Since she loves him, she *must* leave him, while he holds opposite view: "'If you love me you can't leave me'" (124). It is Lydia, who ironically discards her first marriage for love, who cannot see that love is a viable reason for marriage – she is incapable of seeing beyond her principles.

What compounds the covert irony here even further is the complication of considering Gannett's needs as an artist. Lydia exploits these needs unconsciously, to further her own unconventionality, and to simultaneously further her fulfillment of social expectation.   When they arrive at the hotel, Gannett again feels artistic stirrings. Lydia sees herself as both his muse and his helpmeet: "He stood before her with the vivid preoccupied stare of the novelist on the trail of a subject: with a relief that was half painful she noticed that, for the first time since they had been together, he was hardly aware of her presence" (112). If he's not aware of her, he won't again confront her with the marriage question, and she will not have to wrestle with it.

There is, then, a huge degree of self-delusion in her supportiveness, because such willingness to allow Gannett to pursue his writing allows her to put the crucial issue of their relationship into stasis. " 'I see a dozen threads," he says, "that already one might follow –'" We see here the first inkling that art and love might, indeed, be mutually exclusive (112). How different this is from the situation in "A Muse's Tragedy." Mary Anerton involves herself in Rendle's art, but remains ever detached from his love – here it is the opposite: Lydia is separate from Gannett's artistic production, but receives all of his love. Penelope Vita-Finzi suggests that with this dichotomy Wharton illustrates arguments for and against an artist's marrying, by presenting three themes that we see here and elsewhere: first, the writer's need for "variety," for a dynamic environment, including the people in it (Vita-Finzi 102-103). Second is the need for, as well as the means of obtaining time, even from one's lover, and third, that one's muse can be both the means of achieving success and the cause for failure (Vita-Finzi 102-

103). The implicit idea here is that writers are motivated by selfishness, and not by morality. A lack of stability, whether financial or social, is distracting and therefore destructive for the artist; the social stability and order of marriage would, therefore, free him (103-104). Gannett thus argues for marriage, Lydia against, and against conformity to social conventions, while Gannett is for compromising with them (103). Gannett is more of a real politic pragmatist: "One may believe in them or not; but as long as they do rule the world it is only by taking advantage of their protection that one can find a *modus vivendi*" (Wharton 111).

Furthermore, Lydia feels a certain degree of guilt and culpability: Gannett has not written a word since running away with her. His love of her has interrupted his artistic production and Lydia recognizes the overt irony of this:

> there was a special irony in the fact, since his passionate assurances that only the stimulus of her companionship could bring out his latent faculty had almost given the dignity of a 'vocation' to her course: there had been moments when she had felt unable to assume, before posterity, the responsibility of thwarting his career. And, after all, he had not written a line since they had been together: his first desire to write had come from renewed contact with the world! (113)

Lydia here, and throughout the story wavers between self-analysis and self-understanding. She could delude herself that her very presence helps him to write, since he declares this to be true – but in this moment of self-understanding, she realizes that he is just saying this. There is a subtler irony in her recognition of the truth. And when he comes again into contact with society and his artistic "itching" begins, her "vocation" switches; Lydia rationalizes his withdrawal from her because of the marriage question. The overt irony is in what she sees about herself here. But more covertly, there is a hidden irony in this new delusion:

> His sudden impulse of activity so exactly coincided with her own wish to withdraw, for a time, from the range of his observation, that she wondered if he too were not seeking sanctuary from intolerable problems. "You must begin tomorrow!" she cried,

hiding a tremor under the laugh with which she added, "I wonder if there's any ink in the inkstand?" (113)

Now she will withdraw from him, again, not because of emotional reasons, but rather, she rationalizes, to become the facilitator for his artistic production: "hiding the tremor under the laugh" from him, and from herself (113). Lydia conveniently re-labels his motives to keep from feeling injured, hurt, and isolated by his withdrawal. She is honest enough with herself to admit that her presence impedes his writing. However, she is unable to see that, in becoming his champion for both his and her withdrawal, ostensibly so that he may write, she unwittingly advocates emotional withdrawal from the earlier crucial issue of marriage, the real issue she refuses to confront. He loves her, wants to be with her, and is, therefore, happy with the impending divorce, because it will enable them to legalize and sanctify their relationship, and to place it back within the bounds of public convention, and therefore convenience and ease with respect to society. Gannett knows himself enough to accept the simplicity and inconsistency of this stance, although he can be unconventional when it suits him, having running away with her despite her legally married status. He does so for selfish reasons, however, and not, as he puts it, to "found a new system of ethics" (110). Barbara White, in writing on this story, emphasizes here the impossibility of "founding a new ethic" of male-female relationships that are socially unconventional, which is repeatedly tested and proven here and elsewhere in Wharton's stories (158). Gannett loves her, wants to be with her, and wants to legalize and sanctify it in eyes of law and society respectively, in order to get on with the real business of his life, writing.

What is the real business of Lydia's life? Perhaps this is at the root of her indecisiveness. Wharton's society is one in which intellectual women didn't often have vocations independent of husband and family, except in unusual circumstances. Lydia is thus left with the perception of having only two choices: to conform, and therefore be determined and self-less, or to reject social norms and assert her selfhood. Lydia's reason d' etre becomes the principle of self-assertion itself, the most covert irony here being her refusal to acknowledge emotional motives or to act on them regardless of convention, which Lydia takes to the point of absurdity. This renders "Souls Belated" an earlier, but more ambiguous version of "The Reckoning."

Lydia's dilemma is reminiscent of Julia Westall's. Both characters initially embrace unconventionality for its own sake, and Julia's "new ethics" sound distinctly like Lydia's "principles": the only true marriage, Julia might have once argued, is based on the ease by which one might end it, putting primacy on the self: "The new adultery was unfaithfulness to self" (427). Julia thus sees no problem, therefore, with making the "unimportant concession[s] to social prejudice" by marrying Clement Westall (427). But where Julia oversimplifies the marital relationship, Lydia overcomplicates it. Julia is unconscious of her own ironic situation, which the observer narrator nastily reveals to us. Her self-knowledge is limited by her sense of herself as the "predestined victim" of her own principles (432). But however nasty the observer narrator is towards Julia, the distance or separation created by this narrator softens her irony. Ultimately, it is easier to feel sympathetic towards, and not aggravated by Julia, because the observer narrator so obviously scorns her. Also, Julia shows enough self-awareness to see that conventionality and unconventionality are only meaningful terms if there is "an inner law . . . the obligation that love creates . . . being loved as well as loving (436). It is this that Lydia fights against as reasonable grounds for marriage. Lydia is not a Julia Westall, utterly traditional beneath the façade of unconventionality that she drops when the application of her "new ethics" to her own marriage forces her to. Nor is she a Paulina Trant, who in "The Long Run," puts the authenticity and extraordinary nature of her feelings for the man she loves (who is not her husband) above morality or convention altogether. Paulina offers to dedicate her life to her beloved without either the façade or the reality of marriage. Paulina has no doctrines, ethics or principles, no theory of the "general rule," only her own specific case (317).

What makes Lydia much more ironic and perhaps more frustrating a character to contend with is that she wants things both ways. She wants to retain her pose, for her own inner justification and redemption, of principled unconventionality consistent with a general rule or set of new ethics, and she wants to retain her public social position, which is not only defined by, but utterly dependent upon her seeming to be married. And all the while, Lydia denies the "inner obligation that love creates," which Julia recognizes too late, and upon which Paulina stakes all. The story, therefore, has to end in ironic covert instability and ambiguity; Wharton presents us with no resolution to Lydia's problem because to do so would remove the ironic immediacy of the tortuous rout such a decision – to marry or not to marry – is to a mind such as hers. This forces us to ask the question of ourselves: what would we do, in her place? A conventional reading assumes that Lydia ultimately concedes and does marry him; but that Wharton does not actually tell us so leaves a lingering doubt about her choice, perhaps the same doubt that will linger in Lydia's mind, whatever her choice may ultimately be.

That this lack of a resolution is filtered through the third-person narrative consciousness of Gannett, which happens only here in the story, is thus doubly ironic and poignant. Lydia's consciousness is submerged within his, as female intellectuals are generally in Wharton's fiction, is problematic. Here again, perhaps Wharton herself senses that a woman's cause could best be advanced through her male characters, as Barbara White contends (58).

To what extent, then, are Lydia and Gannett souls belated? A conventional interpretation, because it is the obvious one, is that they are souls are belated because they come to each other late, after she's married to another, thus compromising their social position and making it seemingly 'impossible' to be together in a legal, socially acceptable way. Their love for each other as soul mates should transcend convention. But perhaps the most covert, because unstable, irony is the ultimate ambiguity of her decision, because it is tempered by his point of view. Wharton almost creates a domestic retelling of *Hamlet*, to marry or not to marry – but decisiveness comes belatedly; it is too late for us read her motives through her consciousness as revealed by the third-person narration. This is, perhaps deliberate on Wharton's part. In 1899 she had not yet determined her own personal position on the issue of making an acceptable marriage, versus her needs as an artist. Is her fiction of Tillotson and Gannett a parallel for her own complicated relationships with Teddy and Walter Berry? Here too, we may never know.

At first glance, the stories "The Pomegranate Seed," (1931) and "Autres Temps . . ." seem to have little in common. The latter, published in *Xingu* in 1916, just three years after Wharton's own divorce, clearly is a poignant reflection of the societal stance on divorce and remarriage just before and after the turn of the century. "The Pomegranate Seed," on the other hand, is a bona fide ghost story, in which, seemingly, the main center of conflict rests rather simply with a dead wife's haunting of her still-living and remarried husband through the letters she sends from beyond the grave. What, then, do these two stories, one written early in Wharton's career, and the other written later in her career, have in common?

In light of a discussion of irony these two unrelated stories share a significant thread of commonality: they reveal literally and symbolically the hold that the past has on the present. Both of the protagonists in these stories are haunted by their pasts, and fail to create a present unencumbered, whether by the presence of a dead but still-voluble and communicative first wife, as in Charlotte Ashby's case; or by the social mores of a society which, though changed, will not vindicate the divorcee Mrs. Lidcote and readmit her to "polite" society. Both of these characters are, consciously or unconsciously, determined by their respective pasts, and the longer each takes to move from self-delusion to self-recognition and understanding, the more infinitely covert and unstably ironic their respective situations become.

Wharton achieves this infinite, covert and unstable irony in two ways: first, by suppressing a narrative voice altogether, replacing the third-person observer narrator with a third-person limited narration that reads, often, like an interior monologue, the result of which is to create a gap between our view of the characters' fictive reality and their respective views of this reality, doubling the inherent dramatic irony. Second, Wharton spins ironies that are continually undermined, without resolution or fixity of meaning, with the double irony of characters who, when reaching an understanding, ultimately, of the irony of their "real" situations, cannot effect any kind of change. The more self-knowledge each gains, the more self-ironic each becomes in his or her impotence.

D.B. Flynn deems "The Pomegranate Seed" one of the Wharton's stories most pessimistic about the human capacity for happiness (203). The story is about the burden of inheritance, in this instance the domestic inheritance left by a first wife, Elsie Ashby, for her successor Charlotte. But unlike Paulina Anson, who relishes the reminders big and small of the man whose life she lives to preserve in "The Angel at the Grave," Charlotte initially refuses to even recognize that any burden of remembrance exists. She has, she believes, "made" things "her own": not only the house and drawing room, but the children and husband as well (Wharton 763). Paulina Anson inhales deeply the vapors of the past that subsumes her own present and future, but Charlotte does just the opposite, denying its and Elsie's hold, even on the house itself: "Even on the occasion of her only visit to the first Mrs. Ashby . . . she had looked about her with an innocent envy, feeling it to be exactly the drawing room she would have liked for herself, and now for more than a year it had been hers to deal with as she chose" (763-764). Architectural interiors in Wharton's fiction represent psychological or emotional interiors, and it is here that Wharton sets the ironic scene. To Charlotte, her drawing room is a "tiny islet," a sanctuary from "the heart of the hurricane" of daily existence that she has "made her own by moving furniture about and adding more books, another lamp, [and] a table for the new reviews"(763). To us, however, the drawing room is completely dominated by the accoutrements of a dead woman: neither "furniture nor hangings had been changed" (764). Charlotte has not only begun "their new life in the old setting," she has taken on the role, the very life, as well as ownership of the objects of her predecessor, looking over "her stepchildren's copybooks," or waiting for "her husband's step" in the very environment and in the very manner in which Elsie used to do these same things (764).

Of course Charlotte does not see herself living out the life of another. She is, at first, quite happy with her life and her marriage. She is confident, thinking of herself as a "sophisticated woman" who "had few illusions about the intricacies of the human heart" (766). Even when given license to renovate, she changes little, feeling "almost sorry" that the one decorative change her husband insists upon is to move Elsie's portrait out of the library and into the nursery (767). Only later does Charlotte admit to herself that Elsie's "banishment," as she guiltily thinks of it, makes her more comfortable in what is, after all, her own home, "since that long coldly beautiful face on the library wall no longer followed her with guarded eyes" (767). Charlotte, dominated by her husband's past, convinces herself that she is "sovereign" over it.

Even her own view of herself as a properly compliant wife reveals the depth of her self-delusion. Charlotte deems even the act of sitting alone in her drawing room as "another way of being with Kenneth, thinking over what he had said when they parted in the morning, imagining what he would say when he sprang up the stairs" (764). In this, she merely succeeds in being Elsie's polar opposite, positing herself as Kenneth's "liberator" from an excessively pushy and demanding first wife. Charlotte allows him to make the decisions and have most of the control in their relationship, or so she thinks, such as when he "hints" passive-aggressively about "some criticism of her household arrangements" (765). Whether she realizes it or not, Charlotte not only picks up where Elsie left off, she also defines herself by being what Elsie was not. Elsie, it would appear, is in control of more than just the decoration of the house.

How peculiar, then, that Charlotte is not the person being haunted, as in a typically suspenseful ghost story. When the mysterious letters appear, they are entirely Kenneth's, not hers; indeed, only Kenneth can make intelligible their faint scrawl, and he does so in utter isolation from her each time a letter appears: "Evidently, whatever the letter contained, he wanted to be by himself to deal with it; and when he reappeared he looked years older, looked emptied of life and courage, and hardly conscious of her presence" (765). Kenneth is, at first, the Persephone figure in the story (Waid 195). Nothing in this house or this marriage truly belongs to Charlotte, not the husband, the children nor the furniture, and not even its ghost. Conventionally the ghost would, we would expect, drive out the unwanted interloper in one way or another, if the author's intention were to scare or to create a Poe-like suspense in the story. This ghost, however, already has what she wants when the story opens, the full attention of and a connection to her husband unbreakable by mere mortality, or by another woman. Elsie, therefore, cannot be bothered with the interloper herself. "You know Elsie Ashby absolutely dominated him," people warned Charlotte before the marriage, and she dominates him still (765). But Charlotte can only recognize flashes of the truth of this, passing off such moments as humorous banter. She jokes as she calls herself his liberator, and again later, in a conversation in which Kenneth refuses to reveal the author or contents of the newly arrived letter: "'I have never forgotten Elsie,' he said. Charlotte could not repress a faint laugh. 'Then, you poor dear, between the three of us'"(773). Wharton's genius here is to manipulate conventional dramatic irony: Charlotte discusses Elsie here as though she still has a say in things, never allowing to float up to the surface of her consciousness the fact that Elsie really does.

We, of course, guess almost immediately the identity of the letters' author, because every descriptive visual cue, as well as Charlotte's recalling of warning words before her wedding, point to Elsie. If Charlotte were simply oblivious to the cues, Charlotte herself would not be ironic, only her situation would. But that Charlotte is conscious, on whatever level, of Elsie's hold on their lives, and can only express an acknowledgement of this reality through self-conscious and sarcastic half-jokes, makes her the object of her own irony, both to us and to herself. While her words hit squarely on the truth of the matter, the tone of these words, a "half joke" or a "faint laugh" undercuts them as she speaks them, allowing Charlotte, paradoxically, to simultaneously see reality and deny what is right in front of her. She is so entangled in her refusal to become fully and un-jokingly conscious of the ghost's identity and what this revelation would mean for herself and her marriage that she asserts to Kenneth that she would rather live with the disturbing letters than live without him, without even knowing their author or contents:

> If I'd seen that the letters made you happy, that you were watching eagerly for them, counting the days between their coming, that you wanted them, that they gave you something I haven't known how to give – why . . . I don't say I shouldn't have suffered from that too; but it would have been in a different way, and I should have had the courage to hide what I felt, and the hope that someday you'd come to feel about me as you did about the writer of those letters. (777-778)

She is willing, for the moment, to utterly subsume her own happiness in his, willing to sacrifice her present and future with him, by sharing him indefinitely with the mysterious letter writer. The more certainty that Charlotte feels about her "victorious" control of her situation, the more unstable and covert the dramatic irony becomes (775). Thinking that the letter write is simply another old flame of Kenneth's, Charlotte persuades him, she believes, to go away with her:

> the secret influence – as to which she was still so completely in the dark – would continue to work against her, and she would have to renew the struggle day after day till they started on their journey. But after that everything would be different. If once she could get her husband away under other skies, and all to herself, she never doubted her power to release him from the evil spell he was under. (779)

Cleverly Wharton uses limited narration here to put us directly into Charlotte's thoughts, so that we feel how strong her confidence is, while simultaneously and contradictorily we know the extent of her delusion. She thinks that "she had faced the phantom and dispelled it," while we know that her figurative phantom is, in fact, a real one. This variance created by the dramatic irony widens with each piece of knowledge Charlotte gains, doubling the irony and its instability. Paradoxically, because her certainty stems from how close to the truth she has come, the closer she comes to recognizing who "that woman" writing the letters is, the further Charlotte gets from understanding her identity. Learning that he has gone out of town without telling her just before they were due to leave together, Charlotte glances into her mirror:

> Of course he had gone to see that woman – no doubt to get her
> permission to leave. He was as completely in bondage as that;
> and Charlotte had been fatuous enough to see the palms of victory
> on her forehead. She burst into a laugh and, walking across the
> room, sat down again before her mirror. What a different face she
> saw! The smile on her pale lips seemed to mock the rosy vision of
> the other Charlotte (780).

How covertly ironic that just as Charlotte reaches the brink of self-recognition, she reaches it at the moment when she literally does not recognize her own reflection, feeling self-alienation at the gaze reflected back at her in the mirror. Wharton then undermines this irony with another, the return of her confident self-delusion: "But gradually her color crept back. After all, she had a right to claim the victory, since her husband was doing what she wanted, not what the other woman exacted of him" (780). Later talking over her plans with her mother-in-law, Charlotte "regain[s] her own self-confidence, her conviction that nothing could ever come again between Kenneth and herself" (781). We almost choke on the irony of this feeling of hers, in particular when Mrs. Ashby invokes Elsie's ghost: "Elsie hated traveling; she was always finding pretexts to prevent his going anywhere. With you, thank goodness, it's different" (781). Her words serve to undermine Charlotte's confidence in two ways; first, by reiterating to us that everyone defines her by being what Elsie was not. Second, Mrs. Ashby's words undercut Charlotte's delusions by the accuracy of their unconscious prophecy, and the fixity of long-held habits: Elsie always had found any way to keep Kenneth with her, and with his disappearance, she still does.

Indeed, Mrs. Ashby plays an interesting role in the story. Though her "astringent bluntness of speech" Mrs. Ashby functions as Charlotte's mouthpiece, giving voice to Charlotte's unsayable thoughts, and bringing the departed Elsie into the foreground. For example, Mrs. Ashby is quick to comment on the removal of Elsie's portrait from the library: "'Elsie gone, eh?'" adding, at Charlotte's murmured explanation: 'Nonsense. Don't have her back. Two's company.' Charlotte, at this reading of her thoughts, could hardly refrain from exchanging a smile of complicity with her mother-in-law" (775). No proper delicacy here – Mrs. Ashby, overtly truthful and consciously forthright in her choice of words, and therefore not consciously ironic, becomes a character who is covertly ironic when she provides clues to the mystery that go unheeded by Charlotte.

Mrs. Ashby thus becomes the ironic index of Charlotte's self-delusion. Wharton, subtle as ever, uses Mrs. Ashby to remind us of Elsie's presence in the house sparingly, avoiding the overt and the obvious, and thereby serving to reveal the extent of Charlotte's obliviousness. Mrs. Ashby's general grasp of Elsie's ongoing role widens the gap between the characters' understanding of their situation and ours, ironically undercutting Charlotte's contradictory alternation between awareness and dimness. For it is only when the truthful and forthright Mrs. Ashby becomes evasive that Charlotte herself can face the truth, as they examine the next letter together, and Charlotte immediately notices that Mrs. Ashby has recognized the handwriting on the letter: "You'd better say it out, mother! You knew at once it was *her* writing? . . . You've answered me now! You're looking straight at the wall where her picture used to hang!" (787). In a covertly ironic reversal Mrs. Ashby solidifies Charlotte's moment of illumination by being unlike her normal self, avoiding the truth even as she is literally facing it. Charlotte finally puts the truth into words:

> Why shouldn't I say it, when even the bare walls cry it out? What difference does it make if her letters are illegible to you and me? If even you can see her face on the blank wall, why shouldn't he read her writing on this blank paper? Don't you see that she's everywhere in this house, and the closer to him because to everyone else she's become invisible? (787)

Finally Charlotte understands, not just the truth of the ghost's identity, but also, and more importantly, the truth of her own situation, and to what extent her own identity is determined, not by her own will, but by that of another. Thus Elsie herself becomes more than just a supernatural figure whose "implausible" presence fuels the plot of the story (*Contemporary Reviews* 534). Elsie is, as D.B. Flynn calls her, the "arbiter of truth," truth not merely about Kenneth's undying attachment to his first wife, but the truth about Charlotte's powerlessness and lack of self-identity, despite her previous delusions of self-autonomy (Flynn 205).

And even after this moment of crisis and subsequent illumination, how does Charlotte respond? "Through all her tossing anguish, Charlotte felt the impact of that resolute spirit [Mrs. Ashby's]" and at Mrs. Ashby's bidding, rises to notify the police that Kenneth is missing, " 'Exactly as if we thought it could do any good to do anything'" (788). To what extent, then, has Charlotte gained self-knowledge? Is acting as the devoted wife to a man who loves another merely an act of compassion towards her mother-in-law? Is it courageous and self-sacrificing, or defiant and rebellious, to continue to behave as if Kenneth were returning? Perhaps her action can be read, as Barbara White does, as a moment of problematic female triumph, turning the story into a "searching – and searing – feminist analysis of the construction of 'femininity'" (White 164). But this is somewhat problematic. Letting Kenneth go would, for Charlotte, mean accepting the irreversible grip that the past, embodied by Elsie, has upon her; but it would also mean, paradoxically, that in accepting and reconciling herself to the hold of the past on the present, she would put herself and self-preservation first. When Charlotte does the opposite, going on, however defiantly, as if she and not another were in control, while simultaneously denying the hold the past has on the present, she gains self-knowledge, admitting finally " 'that everything,'" even the impossible, " 'is possible'" as she says to Mrs. Ashby (787). Charlotte is simultaneously self-ironic and self-subsumed. But her understanding this is to no effect – nothing in Charlotte's life promises to change or improve because of this knowledge. She traps herself, ironically, in the past that she refuses to acknowledge. This is why this story, like "Souls Belated," ends in ambiguity: we do not ultimately know if Kenneth is alive or dead, or whether the ghost or Charlotte has prevailed. To answer these questions, Wharton would have had to write an ending that proclaimed a female 'victor,' as Barbara White suggests, a form of female vengeance though the victory itself is imperfect (White 99). But whose victory would it be? One woman's, at the cost of another's? To read this story only as a feminist restructuring of the Persephone myth is an oversimplification, because Kenneth, though certainly a victim, is not Elsie's only victim, nor is he the story's protagonist; Charlotte is. It is perhaps the infinitely unstable and covert irony that Wharton derives from not resolving the story to the advantage of one woman over another that enables her to deal with feminist issues relevant to her, while not claiming herself to be a feminist.

Equally complex beneath the surface of its relatively simple plot is the story "Autres Temps . . ." (1916). Like "The Pomegranate Seed," "Autres Temps . . ." is a story in which the most infinitely unstable and covert irony stems from the story's lack of a clear resolution, and from the third-person limited narration of the protagonist, which creates a variance between her understanding of things and ours. Furthermore this use of increasingly covert and unstable irony enables Wharton to wrestle with ideologically charged themes and issues, while not ultimately taking a clear stance on any one side.

"Autres temps . . . autres moeurs": manners do change with the times, and Mrs. Lidcote learns this lesson in this unrelenting story. She is who Lydia in "Souls Belated" might have become a generation earlier, without a man or the pretense of marriage, living expatriated in Italy and returning home to New York as the story opens, isolated, alone, "frozen in time" (Flynn 169). Mrs. Lidcote is every bit as caught in the grip of the ghost of her own past choices as Charlotte is, with even more ironic weight (169). If ghost stories, as Barbara White contends, were Wharton's medium for "say[ing] the unsayable," then Wharton, through the "ghost" of Mrs. Lidcote's past, says quite an earful about society's hypocrisy, and the betrayal of mothers by daughters (White 164). The story first appeared in *Xingu* in 1916, just three years after Wharton's own divorce of Teddy, to many laudatory reviews. One reviewer calls the story "clever, penetrating, implying far more and touching inferentially on issues far broader than those bearing on the fortunes of Mrs. Lidcote and the daughter who followed in her footsteps" (*Contemporary Reviews* 227). As contemporary critics point out, the story deals with dichotomies of male-female behaviors, of old New York and new, of mothers and daughters, of social customs versus individual desires, and of mass versus high culture, all of which are themes inherent in the best of Wharton's fiction (Bauer 8-12; Brown 77).

Another dichotomy in the story is irony itself. On one level, the ironic content reads as Wharton at her most obvious, overt, and stable: characters state clearly that they see their situations as ironic, and have self-awareness, and titles and names, such as the title of the story itself, or the name of the ship, the "Utopia," upon which Mrs. Lidcote has sailed to New York, have more covert but limited and local ironic interpretations. The plot of the story is obviously ironic, stable, and simple. Mrs. Lidcote, a divorcee when divorce automatically condemned one to be a social pariah in the upper social strata of New York, has spent eighteen years abroad. Now she is returning to her daughter, also a divorcee, but successfully remarried – "'Leila? Oh, *Leila's* all right'" – despite the "dark inheritance" Mrs. Lidcote "had bestowed upon her daughter" (Wharton 258). This character shows Wharton at her most overtly ironic as the former thinks over her situation, pondering the irony of how the fates have shorn the threads of her life: "Certainly it was a master stroke of those arch-ironists of the shears and spindle to duplicate her own story in her daughter's" (258). Only a shade less overt is the irony of the predictable outcome of the story: that though society accepts her daughter and her marital choices, society will never accept Mrs. Lidcote's, as she admits to her long-time admirer Franklin Ide. She has "never noticed – the least change – in [her] own case" (261). Her daughter Leila, who at first is overly effusive in her welcome of her mother, immediately proceeds to hide her away from other weekend company whom her presence would offend. Mrs. Lidcote's awareness of this situation unfolds as the story progresses: "'I was stupid . . . I ought to have gone to Ridgefield with Susy. I didn't see till afterward that I was expected to"(277). No "new dispensation" had come in her case, and Mrs. Lidcote recognizes just how ironic this is, saying to Franklin Ide

> It's simply that society is much too busy to revise its own judgments. Probably no one in the house with me stopped to consider that my case and Leila's were identical. The only remembered that I'd done something which, at the time I did it, was condemned by society. (279)

Here, as earlier, Mrs. Lidcote expresses her understanding of the covert but stable irony of her situation directly to her audience in first person. According to M.M. Brown, we see irony in the 'new' values, represented by Leila, that are not retroactive for Mrs. Lidcote (Brown 77). Barbara White reads Mrs. Lidcote as a prisoner of her consciousness of her past (88). Indeed, both Mrs. Lidcote and Charlotte have self-perception and their consciousness of the irony of their respective situations makes their choices self-sacrifices, Charlotte to go on as though her husband would return to their "happy" marriage, and Mrs. Lidcote to return, alone, to Florence. Mrs. Lidcote has tried her own old case against a new society, and lost. This is barely covertly ironic and utterly stable, for the story allows for little misinterpretation of the hypocrisy inherent in the inexorability of society's judgment upon her.

However if the contemporaneous *New York Times* reviewer was correct, there are greater issues at stake in this story than Mrs. Lidcote's situation itself. That Wharton's characters so rarely announce the irony inherent in their situations should make this kind of irony immediately suspicious and therefore ironic itself. For underlying this irony is a more covert, unstable ironic subtext: Wharton tells Mrs. Lidcote's story, and through it, questions the broader issue of the relationship of the individual to society, and to other individuals in a modern, and therefore different, world, questions that are particularly prevalent in American literary culture precisely when Wharton wrote this story. "Autres Temps. . .", presaging Wharton's late short fiction, which is criticized as inferior because cruel and ruthless towards its characters and their situations, is unrelenting in allowing Mrs. Lidcote no alternatives: her past has imprisoned her present and future happiness (White 88). In her portrayal of Mrs. Lidcote, a woman whose entire life, present and future, has been determined by a past that rejects and isolates her, Wharton, herself no modernist in terms of experimental technique nor an advocate of the "New Woman" ethos prevalent in the Jazz age, comes as close as she ever will to experimenting with a modernist sensibility – to read her as simply opposed to modernist ideas is an oversimplification (Barrish 97). We see this sensibility in her rejection of the past for the present, a sense of cultural uncertainty post World War I, a sense that language is inadequate for meaningful human communication, and that therefore the potential for significant human relationships has dwindled. Frequently Wharton's stories reveal a modernist, not romantic "spiritual emptiness" (Singley, "Edith Wharton's Ironic Realism 239). We can read Mrs. Lidcote as a female Prufrock (though in literary fact predating Eliot's by a year) because of her age, her hesitation and timidity in the world around her, and in her difficulty in understanding the present in which she finds herself:

The past was bad enough, but the present and future were worse,

> because they were less comprehensible, and because, as she grew
> older, surprises and inconsequences troubled her more than the
> worst certainties …in the present fluid state of manners what did
> anything imply except what their hats implied – that no one could
> tell what was coming next? (Wharton 258-259)

Mrs. Lidcote's words often echo Eliot's Prufrock's; Prufrock staggers under the weight of trivialities, inconsequentials: "Shall I part my hair behind? Do I dare to eat a peach?" (l.122). Manners are social cues, and Mrs. Lidcote, belonging to a time with different manners, has no vocabulary with which to read the new ones she finds waiting for her. Like Prufrock, she sees people "come and go," but they, like Prufrock's mermaids, do not sing to her. Cut off from all social interaction, she admits, "Yes, yes; I'm happy. But I'm lonely, too – lonelier than ever. I didn't take up much room in the world before; but now – where is there a corner for me?" (Wharton 264). The deeper, more covert irony in the story is not merely the hypocritical discrepancy between society's reaction to her daughter versus its reaction to herself, but rather it is Wharton's modernistic questioning: the difficulty of reading the cues of society, the problem of interpretation itself in a world in which all previously known signs have become detached from their conventional signifiers. Mrs. Lidcote finds that the very structure of people's conversations have changed since she's been abroad: "Their talk leaped elliptically from allusion to allusion, their unfinished sentences dangled over bottomless pits of conjecture" (259). How similar this sentiment is to Prufrock's: "It is impossible to say just what I mean!" (l.104). We hear it again in Frost's "Home Burial," in the anguish of a grieving father and husband: "My words are nearly always an offense. /I don't know how to speak of anything" (l.48-49). Wharton taps into the modernists' feeling that language is an insufficient medium for meaningful human interaction, but at the same time she criticizes this idea, speaking through Mrs. Lidcote's third-person limited ruminations on the bit of conversation she has overheard about her daughter. She thinks to herself that "they gave their bewildered hearer the impression not so much of talking only of their intimates as of being intimate with everyone alive" (Wharton 259). That is, that this 'new' fragmented method of communicating assumes an understanding not just of the specific social set of "idle and opulent people" whom Mrs. Lidcote overhears on the voyage to New York, but paradoxically, individuals in general (259). How, Wharton implicitly questions, can a writer represent the subjective perceptions of an individual, which he or she claims is the only means of representing human experience, while then generalizing that every individual subjectively perceives the world in the same way? Dale Bauer asserts that one of Wharton's assets as a writer his her ability to "think against herself," "interrogating" alternative values and principles, which allows her not only to take a critical stance against modern culture but to reveal its limitations (9). Thus we have a character, Mrs. Lidcote, who is ironic in two ways simultaneously, because she is covertly both the culture critic, and more overtly its victim. This allows Wharton, by representing in her the "old America," to question it while also challenging the values of "new America" that replaces the old (Bauer 12). In Wharton's fiction in general, and in particular in this story the protagonist searches not only for societal approbation and acceptance, but also for authentic emotional experience (17-18). Mrs.Lidcote, caught between old and new, much like Wharton herself, is ambivalent and draws no final conclusions about the new society that, like the old, rejects her (18). The modernists searched for a new kind of order in a world they saw as profoundly disordered, positing art as the place in which reordering might occur successfully. Wharton is highly skeptical of the modernist agenda, emphasizing the fictionality of fiction, in which even there an ordered world is not possible. "The huge threat" of chaotic New York is for Mrs. Lidcote a "sphinx whose riddle she must read or perish" (Wharton 263, 260). Her very survival depends upon her interpretive potential. But Mrs. Lidcote wonders,

> where indeed in this crowded, topsy-turvey world, with its
> headlong changes and helter-skelter readjustments, its new
> tolerances and indifferences and accommodations, was there room
> or a character fashioned by slower sterner processes and a life

> broken under their inexorable pressure? And then, in a flash, she
> viewed the chaos from a new angle, and order seemed to move
> upon the void. (Wharton 267)

A more overt irony lies in Mrs. Lidcote's hope that society, having undergone a "general readjustment" with "bolder freer harmonies" would readmit her to its ordered ranks, allowing her to believe in a future with Frank Ide (267). But more covertly ironic is Wharton's dialogue with modernist philosophy, in which she uses its own language against itself in Mrs. Lidcote's thoughts, words like "chaos," "order," and "tiny fragment" (267). Wharton manipulates and exploits modernist language and themes subtly to generate the covert irony that her protagonist believes that she might achieve individual happiness – by becoming a Lydia, rather than a Paulina Trant – while still recognizing that society is not ready to accept her. But Franklin Ide is.

At first Ide seems to be his own man, not one to be held back by conventions of the past, despite his keeping with the certain "old New York" traditions, such sending up a box of long white-stemmed roses before calling on his friend:

> She was sure he had felt sorry for her, sorrier perhaps than anyone
> had ever felt; but he had always paid her the supreme tribute of not
> showing it. His attitude allowed her to imagine that compassion
> was not the basis of his feeling for her, and it was part of her joy in
> his friendship that it was the one relation seemingly unconditional
> by her state, the only one in which she could think and feel and
> behave like any other woman. (259-260)

Certainly it is covertly ironic that Mrs. Lidcote feels herself to be a "functioning female" only in the company of this man; often in the short fiction we see Wharton introducing women's issues through male characters, and we see both her engagement with and skepticism of feminist ideology here, since the women in Mrs. Lidcote's life, especially her own daughter, fail her. In fact, it is Ide, and not she, who correctly reads the new social scene. Mrs. Lidcote discusses her sense of urgency in reaching Leila after her speedy divorce and immediate remarriage:

> "She may dislike the idea of seeing people." Ide, whose
> absent shortsighted gaze had been fixed on the slowly gliding
> water turned in his seat to stare at his companion.
> "Who? Leila?" he said with an incredulous laugh . . . his
> look grew gently commiserating. "I think you'll find –" he paused
> for a word – "that things are different now – altogether easier."
> (260)

And it is Franklin Ide, not Mrs. Lidcote, who first recognizes the reality of her
position with respect to society. He reiterates what she has already overheard
aboard ship: Leila and her husband are "all right" (261). But he goes on to point
out that "it would take an arbitration commission a good many sittings to define
the boundaries of society nowadays. But at any rate they're in New York; and I
assure you you're *not;* you're farther and farther away from it" (261). Only then
can Mrs. Lidcote admit to him and to herself that she's "never noticed the least
change – in" her "own case" (261). Even her cousin Susy Suffern, who "used to
represent Old New York" informs her, Julia Westall-like, "that every woman had
the right to happiness and that self-expression was the highest duty" and that she
misunderstood Leila: "she said my point of view was conventional!" (263). Ide,
and to a lesser extent, Susy Suffern, becomes both Mrs. Lidcote's bridge between
old and new social mores, and the guide who attempts to lead her across the way.

Franklin Ide had befriended her in Switzerland eight years before, "and
then, just at the end, in his odd indirect way, he had let her see that it rested with
her to have him stay" (265). He pled his love for her indirectly then, and renews it
again indirectly: 'There's something I want to say to you,' he began" (265).
Wharton here, as elsewhere in her short fiction, uses indirection herself, leaving
his statement incomplete, save for her filtered version of what he may or may not
have said. The dash, of which the story is full, becomes a trope for the unstated,
and is weighed with ironic significance. We never hear a proposal in Ide's own
voice, only that he has hinted at one. She ruminates, while being ignored by her
daughter, on this hinted-at proposal throughout the rest of the story, again

"overwhelmed at the senseless waste of her own adventure, and wrung with the irony of perceiving that the success or failure of the deepest human experiences may hang on a matter of chronology" (268). Mrs. Lidcote recognizes the irony of her own stance with her past, that her isolation from society and her daughter was a needless sacrifice to the dead gods of propriety and convention; it is her statement of recognition of irony and self-understanding that makes her more overtly ironic. The more profound covert irony here occurs with Mrs. Lidcote's misunderstanding of how tight the grip of the past will be on her future, daring to hope that a future with Franklin Ide will be redemptive of her past. Asking permission to call upon her the night before his trip to Chicago, he brings up the subject of marriage again, as we learn through her consciousness, "directly this time, and in such a form that she could not evade it: putting the renewal of his plea, after so long an interval, on the ground that, on her only showing, her chief argument against it no longer existed" (266). He expresses, she tells us, a "shy deliberateness that, even to Mrs. Lidcote's troubled perceptions, sounded a long-silenced note of feeling. Perhaps the breaking down of the barrier of reticence between them had released unsuspected emotions in both"(263). How covertly ironic that at the instant he lays bare for her the truth of the matter, that she is in every way out of touch with the new value system of society, (and she admits that its position toward her has not yet changed), that this is also the instance in which her hope for a future with Ide is born. But we only experience his "long silenced note of feeling" through *her* consciousness; it is again only through her thoughts, and not his direct voice, that we learn of his marriage proposals. Wharton does this in much the same way that she has Mary Anerton suppress Danyers' voice and marriage proposal in "The Temperate Zone," in her letter to him. However in "Autres Temps . . ." we have no letters – only Mrs. Lidcote's consciousness as the touchstone to reality, controlling as Mary Anerton does, only much more decisively, our perception of Ide's emotional state. Here, as in "The Temperate Zone," we must question whether this potential is fact or mere self-delusion.

Wharton utterly destabilizes our notions of "objective fictive reality" vis-à-vis Mrs. Lidcote's consciousness, challenging the effectiveness of representing subjective reality in fiction by the very act using it. Wharton implies that truth and knowledge are never absolute – that they are accessible only through indirection or subjective consciousness, if at all, that its very subjectivity challenges its status as real.

Ide plays a further, even more important role than representing a potential for a loving and significant relationship: he represents Mrs. Lidcote's very sense of self: he "helped her to hold fast to her identity in the rush of strange names and new categories that her cousin's talk poured out on her" (266). But in order for Mrs. Lidcote, who has paid with the best years of her life for the theft of the happiness that her daughter's contemporaries were taking as their due," to take *her* due, she must reinvent herself, or, to quote Ezra Pound, to make herself "new," living in the present moment only and utterly divorcing herself from her past history unless she find a means of exploiting it for her own purposes. But even if she could, no one, including her own daughter, would allow her to do so, not permitting her any social intercourse during her enforced "two day's seclusion" (275).

> "They won't think it odd if I don't appear?"
> "Oh, not in the least, dearest. I assure you they'll *all* understand." Leila . . . turned back to her mother, her face alight with reassurance. Mrs. Lidcote stood motionless, her head erect, her smiling eyes on her daughter's.
> "Will they think it odd if I *do*? (274)

Both Mrs. Lidcote and Leila are fully aware of the significance of this statement, the latter relieved and embarrassed by her relief that her pariah-mother will not with her "old self" appear to inconvenience her or insult her guests. Mrs. Lidcote, however, understands that she cannot simply throw aside her past – its residue clings forever. Tacitly Wharton admonishes the modernists' discarding of their literary past; art, like identity, cannot simply abandon the past by severing itself

from it: definition, even by negation, is nevertheless still definition. "My case,"
Mrs. Lidcote says to Ide,

> Has been passed on and classified: I'm the woman who has been
> cut for nearly twenty years. The older people have half-forgotten
> why, and the younger ones have never really known: it's simply
> become a tradition to cut me. And traditions that have lost their
> meaning are the hardest of all to destroy. (279)

Mrs. Lidcote understands the more overt irony that her position in society has not
nor will never change. The "tradition" of social rejection may have lost its
meaning, but in an unresolvable paradox, it is cemented into societal behavior
towards her in perpetuity, and she has "lost any illusions" about escaping the
"little tight round of habit and association" into which society has placed her. But
when Ide figuratively offers to share this imprisonment, she seems, ultimately, to
reject the very possibility of his doing so, speaking as much about the nature of
and potential for individual subjective experience as about herself: "We're all
imprisoned, of course – all of us middling people, who don't carry our freedom in
our brains. But we've accommodated ourselves to our different cells, and if we're
moved suddenly into the new ones we're likely to find a stone wall where we
thought there was thin air, and to knock ourselves against it" (279).

Thus while Wharton seems to agree with the modernists' pessimism about
human potential for happiness in relationships, it is Mrs. Lidcote's past itself that
creates this impossibility, and no amount of severing herself from the past will
redeem her sense of self, or self-freedom. For despite Ide's urging that they be
together, he is willing to enter a relationship only if outside of and away from
New York society – he does not admit her reentrance to society, even literally:
"Why shouldn't we go down and see Margaret Wynn for half an hour?". . . "Oh,
no – not tonight!' he exclaimed" (280). And he continues making excuses for why
she should remain in seclusion, just as Susy and Leila did, hypocritically just
seconds after urging her not to be afraid "of them." Her dispensation from society
to be with Ide when once she could not even broach the possibility, only comes at

the cost of continued expatriation and social isolation: "We'll talk of this in Florence soon" (280). But Mrs. Lidcote sees his words as "a painted gauze let down between herself and the real facts of life, and a sudden desire seized her to tear the gauze into shreds" (280). His discussion propels the story to yet another ambiguous ending. They can have a relationship, but only in Florence – do they? Mrs. Lidcote, defined perpetually only by her first marriage, and never graced in the story with a forename, is denied a self-identity. Covertly and unstably ironic is that she can neither get beyond the pale of society, nor exist without it – her personal identity is inextricably tied to a societal context and the history of her past relationships within it. We are given no clues as to whether Mrs. Lidcote renews her relationship with Franklin Ide when she returns to Florence, or even whether society approves or disapproves, and we cannot extrapolate the outcome: to exist without society would make her identity entirely dependent upon his, and neither existing alone nor with him in those circumstances could be entirely satisfactory to Wharton, for whom both art and personal happiness must exist in tandem with – or in dialogic tension with – public acceptance and a past history with which one must come to terms. Wharton herself never remarries, nor does she live entirely within New York society as she posits it in her fiction. Carol Singley suggests that Wharton's later stories, and in particular her ghost stories are moral or spiritual journeys, quests for epistemological solutions (Singley 4). But in this early story, Mrs. Lidcote, haunted by a past that refuses to divorce her, represents for Wharton both the difficulty a woman must have faced in pursuing personal and marital happiness within a context of rigid, if unacknowledged societal conventions, and the failure of an individual to interpret the signs of modernity defined by, but nevertheless rejecting its own past, an infinitely unstable ironic paradox impossible even for Wharton to resolve.

Chapter Four

The "Difference" of Wharton's "Genius"

Most of the change we think we see in life
Is due to truths being in and out of favor.
– Robert Frost, "The Black Cottage"

Robert Frost, in discussing change and our perception of it, uses the word "truths": that is, principles or ideologies that come in and out of favor, in and out of fashion. Two ideas come to mind here – obviously, that identifying what irony is and where we find it is one of those "truths" currently in favor; as many repeatedly point out, irony has been a preoccupation for most of the twentieth century and the beginning of the twenty-first. And although several critics have identified Wharton with irony, no one seems to have sufficiently examined why Wharton used irony so consistently in her short fiction and novels. M. M. Brown posits that Wharton's very philosophy of life was ironic, and that this philosophy forms the thread that connects Wharton's life with her art (Brown 18-19). But this idea presupposes that Wharton's tendency to use irony in the short stories is an unconscious one, and not a deliberate strategy – that she responds to the events in her life with irony spontaneously through her art. This implication of unconscious ironic effect seems disingenuous for several reasons. For example, if one were to undertake the laborious process of cataloguing all of the varied ironic techniques in Wharton's fiction into one comprehensive list, it would be a list rivaling D.C. Muecke's long treatise on the types of irony. Surely the amount of verbal and situational irony found in Wharton's work cannot be merely a result of an unconsciously operative ironic philosophy.

Another reason for questioning the usefulness of this idea is Wharton's artistic philosophy itself, or rather, the loose web of literary ideas one can glean from her various uncollected critical essays, from *The Writing of Fiction* and from her autobiography *A Backward Glance*. She says of style, for example, in *The*

Writing of Fiction that words are the exterior symbols of thought, and it is only by their "exact use that the writer can keep on his subject the close and patient hold which 'fishes the murex up,' and steeps his creation in unfading colours. Style in this definition is discipline, and the self-consecration it demands....for habit makes the style of the writer" (21). Discipline, self-consecration, habit; in other words, the conscious and deliberate choice of words and techniques is Wharton's credo for writers, and one which she reiterates throughout her critical writing, arguing that "patience, meditation, concentration, all the quiet habits of mind now so little practiced, so seldom inculcated" make genius fruitful, and without which it would be "unusable" (71). We can only conclude, therefore, that Wharton applied this credo to herself, utilizing her own "principle of selection" in producing her art ("The Vice of Reading" 105); her use of irony is a crucial part of her craft, and her use of its techniques to create fictional effects is a conscious strategy. As Wharton's biographers have pointed out, the strenuousness of Wharton's adherence to the work habits, the "regularized habits" she established for herself early on in her career reveal her underlying aesthetic of the discipline of the craft (Benstock 25).

That Wharton had an ironic philosophy is an interesting and perhaps provable idea. Useful here is Gary Handwerk's definition of irony as not merely a rhetorical device, but as a philosophical perspective characterized by interrogation, inquisitiveness, "an impulse toward self-reflexiveness" that leads to epistemological questioning (172). Irony, for Wharton, is perhaps a response to and expression of a world in fragments, "the expression of the mind in search of what will suffice" (173). However, this idea does not take us any further to an understanding of why she may have chosen deliberately and repeatedly to employ this philosophy in her short fiction, and perhaps in her long fiction as well. A second idea that Frost's view of truth and change brings to mind is the idea of truth itself being in and out of favor in American letters: that is, the methods and motivations for portraying characters, scenes and situations in art "truly," or authentically, or portraying them as we would like them to be. While I certainly do not mean to suggest that all of American literary history can be condensed into the idealism/realism dichotomy, both of these strains of thought occupy nineteenth-century American literature, and the decline of the former leads to several literary responses, including moralism, sentimentalism, and sensationalism in the popular fiction that was Wharton's literary inheritance.

We might, then, consider Wharton's use of irony, whether or not extending from an ironic world-view, as a deliberate aesthetic strategy that she adopted as a response to and largely a reaction against the aesthetic strategies and choices of those who preceded her, and those with whom she was contemporaneous, for example, the realist writers. Critic Phillip Barrish notes that literary realism creates "cultural distinction," prestige or status: that difference, separateness, was a goal of the realist authors and their characters (5-6). It became a means of reacting to a given reality, while simultaneously maintaining a safe distance from it, and therefore remaining in control of it (7). For example, Wharton's Duchess of Beltishire in *The House of Mirth* champions Lily Bart through accusations of sexual misconduct when the rest of the world shuns her, because she has the social status necessary to distance herself, and thereby ignore outright, social convention (7). Gaining such distinction allowed realist authors both the emotional closeness to and the necessary distance from what the narrative posits as 'real,' social issues such as class, money, sex and death, and linguistic issues such as dialects and use of vernacular speech, and more abstract issues well (3). For many of the realists, including Wharton, 'realism' becomes a strategy for attaining and maintaining literary distinction and status in the face of enormous and unsettling social change: the industrialization, urbanization, immigration and consumerism of the newly-emerging modern world (153n3).

The first group of writers Wharton rejects is the minor "morality" novelists whose roots can be traced to the powerful morality of the Puritans. Puritan moral ideals emerge as Franklinian pragmatism, rational liberalism and humanism in the eighteenth century, and as Emersonian idealism early in the nineteenth century (Stovall 21, 36). But by the middle of the nineteenth century, Emersonian idealism changed somewhat with the changing of external conditions, and especially with the advent of material potential: a coupling of older idealism with materialism, either to justify the latter with the former, or to escape materialism by removing oneself into moral and sentimental idealism. Literature of the middle and late nineteenth century was shaped by popular taste and national ideals; Herbert F. Smith, in *The Popular American Novel 1865-1920*, points out that novelists of this period had many strategies with which "to circumvent, to recondition, or to subvert that popular taste" (Smith preface). No major nineteenth-century American writer was in touch with the dominant ethic of the period: the Protestant ethic (Smith 1). Rather, most felt contempt and distaste for both the ideals and the hypocrisies beneath them – the ethic was a triumvirate of success, reform, and piety. There were several novelists who represented this pyramid of Protestant values, for example, Horatio Alger. Alger's novels focus on success, almost to the point of caricature (2). In *Ragged Dick* (1865), for instance, the Alger hero is the wise but underprivileged boy who rises to success (2-4).

The author representing reform, the second of the three moral strains, is Josaiah Gilbert Holland (2). An Alger hero himself, he is the moralizer of the American public (6). In novels such as *Sevenoaks* (1875), using a black and white villian/heroine formula, Holland shows that reform leads to success and affluence (6). Third in this trio, Edward P. Roe's novels focused on piety (2). Roe was an ordained minister turned writer (130). In *Barriers Burned Away* (1872) and other novels, Roe's hero is a pietist in "Sodom" who rises to success despite temptation, and rescues and converts a misguided heroine (14-15). In his novels we find the best representation of American "genteel" middle-class taste, in which the heroes of Holland and Roe ultimately "out-Alger Alger" (15-16). The "trinity of success, piety and reform under[lies] the action in virtually all of the novels, good, bad, and indifferent" in the period (17). Even Mark Twain was personally influenced by success, Howells by Christian socialism and reform, James by piety and goodness in characters (18). The difference between these three novelists and the rest of the period's novelists is a difference of degree, not of kind: Twain, James and Howells chose drama over melodrama, psychology over "ideality," true sentiment over sentimentality (18).

Though certainly an admirer (though not without reservations) of the latter two, Wharton was generally derisive of the overly moralistic tone and limited subject matter of "the Puritan marionettes," as she scathingly describes them in *A Backward Glance* (127). Commenting on the limitation of the subject matter in several youth's magazines which refused to consider for publication anything dealing with " 'religion, love, politics, alcohol or fairies,'" Wharton quips that "the amusing thing about this turn of the wheel is that we who fought the good fight are now jeered at as the prigs and prudes who barred the way to complete expression – as perhaps we should have tried to do, had we known it was to cause creative art to be abandoned for pathology!" (127). Wharton emphasizes her own aesthetic position against the prudish moralizers in her discussion of Edwin Godkin, an editor of the *New York Evening Post*

> who said that the choice of articles published in American magazines were entirely determined by the fear of scandalizing a non-existent clergyman in the Mississippi Valley; and I made up my mind from the first that I would never sacrifice my literary conscience to this ghostly censor. . . A higher standard of taste in letters can be achieved only if authors will refuse to write down to the particular Mississippi Valley level of today. (*BG* 140)

And refuse is precisely what Wharton did. Of course to say that Wharton thus ignores moral or religious issues in her fiction would be inaccurate. Shari Benstock locates Wharton's moral issues in her childhood, as "moral confusion" between truthfulness and politeness: "Between these two forms of social conduct" – of politeness, her mother's requirement, and being "kind,' her father's – "lay a vast unchartered territory of moral conscience that Edith and her brothers had to map for themselves" (Benstock 23-24). Carol J. Singley's study *Edith Wharton: Matters of Mind and Spirit* (1995) places Wharton's literature within the context of her intellectual and philosophical roots: Calvinism and Catholicism, and classical and modern philosophy. Moral dilemmas abound in her fiction and short fiction, though not necessarily "accentuat[ed]" (Singley 3). In her story "The Lamp of Psyche," for instance, Wharton questions the moral implications surrounding her father's generation of upper-class men who failed to participate in the Civil War, dramatized by Delia Corbett and her husband: " 'Then why weren't you in the war?' she said . . . 'Really,' he said with a smile, 'I don't think I know'" (Wharton 56). Wharton, to reinforce her interest in issues of morality, portrays a female Bostonian version of this Mississippi Valley figure in Aunt Mary Hayne, a reformer, moralist, and general do-gooder, whose purposeful life contrasts sharply with that of her "frivolous" niece Delia, and her seemingly amoral nephew-in-law Corbett, the dilettante around whom Delia's moral problem centers. Aunt Mary is "incurably serious," a person who "never had time to think of her house or her dress" because of "her inflammatory zeal for righteousness in everything from baking powder to municipal government" (48, 49). Clearly, however, Wharton draws a difference between her own profound spiritual and moral quests and the mere scolding parochialism she senses in the "pleaders of special causes," naming in "Permanent Values in Fiction" Harriet Beecher Stowe, Charles Reade, and Elizabeth Gaskell, who, even though considered by Wharton to be the best of this minor, but quite popular group of writers, "simply told their stories in terms of the moral they wanted to enforce, instead of letting their characters follow unhindered the devious ways of experience" (175).

Wharton also despised and rejected the sentimental novel, with its lightening of serious themes, and softening of ideas. Floyd Stovall presents three reasons for the rise of sentimental fiction after the middle of the century. First, traditional religion, such as Calvinism, eases into less harsh forms such as Unitarianism, Transcendentalism, and many "quasi-religions"; for many, reform movements such as the abolition of slavery, or the temperance movement, quench religious thirst ("The Decline of Romantic Idealism" 331). Second, as many men migrate west or become involved in maritime trade, women represented the majority of the population in northeastern America (331). Finally, northern industrialization creates a need, especially for the women populating the factories, for a diversion from the misery of their everyday lives. Thus a taste for escapism in the reading public is born: hugely popular, for example, was the *Godey's Lady's Book* annual, containing "pious romances" (332). Harriet Beecher Stowe's *Uncle Tom's Cabin,* or Caroline Hentz's very different *The Planter's Northern Bride* share a sentimentalized moral idealism (336). Writers such as Susan Warner, Mary Jane Holmes, and Mrs. E.D.E.N Southworth, to name a few exemplars of Hawthorne's " 'mob of scribbling women,'" created stock characters whose sighs, tears, pious actions and rewards for virtue entertained women for decades (332). Hildegarde Hoeller recently argued that Wharton was not only critiquing the sentimental novel, but engaging with it and utilizing it: it gives her, she claims, "an artistic medium to express female passions and desires" making Wharton's sentimental revisions "correc[tive]" of the "limitations of realism" (xii). But this is, perhaps, an oversimplification. Phillip Barrish contends that many of Wharton's characters, such as Nona in *Twilight Sleep,* for example, or Beatrice in the Palmato fragment, represent inclusion in a traumatic and emotionally violent reality (126-157). These female characters become the "conscious bearer[s] of catastrophic knowledge" – real knowledge, rather than artificial emotions, "faced internally," and intellectualized (108, 127). Wharton puts primacy on thoughts, not on feelings (156-157).

Wharton's intense disdain for the sensational sort of fiction, and the American temper that demanded it, appears in several of her short stories, including "The Pelican," in which the amiable Mrs. Amyot, an enthusiastic if not very erudite popular lecturer, has made her living from the gullibility of an audience willing to finance her bathetic situation: she is a widow lacking any other means of supporting her child – "she was 'doing it for the baby," despite the fact that the baby was a grown man! (Wharton 88). We certainly see Wharton's intense dislike of sentimentality in her portrait of Orestes Anson in "The Angel at the Grave," whose literary success is less dependent upon artistic value than upon "one of those anticipated immortalities not uncommon at a time when people were apt to base their literary judgments on their emotions, and when to affect plain food and despise England went a long way toward establishing a man's intellectual pre-eminence" (Wharton 246).

An even more pointed critique of popular sentimental fiction and those who read it occurs in the story "Xingu," (1911) whose "Lunch Club" mocks the proliferation of clubs and societies, especially ladies' societies, whose popularized intellectual efforts and artistic pretensions not only irritate Wharton, but also concern her: she sees that "the limitations of a female audience hindered the growth of all women" (Waid 8). She worries in "Permanent Values in Fiction" that the reading public is "apt to be taken in either by sheer sentimentality, or by what one might call a cultured mediocrity; and if left to himself would swing contentedly between the two" (178). And while admitting a fondness for the "agreeable volumes of travel and art criticism of the cultured dilettante type" by the "cultured amateur," such as Pater's *Renaissance,* and works by Bourget, Symonds, and Vernon Lee, Wharton expresses a "deep contempt for picturesque books about architecture" which "made me side with those who wished to banish sentiment from the study of painting and sculpture" (*BG* 140-141). Indeed, the "mechanical reader," as Wharton formally describes the Lunch Club readers in an essay entitled "The Vice of Reading," is "harmful" for four reasons: first, such readers create the demand for "mediocre writing" and thus "the mediocre author" ("The Vice of Reading" 104). Second, the subsequent "populari[zing]" of "abstruse and difficult subjects" slows down the progress of culture; third, "the harmful book is the trivial book" because it confuses "moral" with "intellectual judgments" (104). Finally, mechanical readers produce even worse offenders, mechanical critics, who become mere "plot extractors" (105). Wharton rejects any association with her "female predecessors," as Carol Singley notes, because ultimately "nineteenth century sentimental virtues worked against the free, open development of critical intelligence which she viewed as women's best opportunity to achieve parity with men" ("Edith Wharton's Ironic Realism" 229).

Wharton dramatizes this critique of sentimental fiction in the story "Xingu" via the amateur Mrs. Leveret, who carries her volume of *Appropriate Allusions* to all meetings of the Lunch Club. Though having "gotten up" Osric Dane, the club is singularly unprepared for the arrival of the great (to them) authoress, who asks contentious questions:

> "The object of our little club . . . is to concentrate the highest
> tendencies of Hillbridge – to centralize and focus its intellectual
> effort . . .We aspire . . .to be in touch with whatever is highest in
> art, literature, and ethics." Osric Dane again turned to her. "What
> ethics?" she asked. A tremor of apprehension encircled the room.
> None of the ladies required any preparation to pronounce on a
> question of morals; but when they were called ethics it was
> different. The club, when fresh from the *Encyclopedia Britannica,*
> the *Reader's Handbook* or Smith's *Classical Dictionary,* could
> deal confidently with any subject ; but when taken unawares it had
> been known to define agnosticism as a heresy of the Early Church
> . . .and such minor members as Mrs. Leveret still secretly regarded
> ethics as something vaguely pagan." (216)

The club members are only saved from the "sting" of Osric Dane's intrusive and embarrassing cross-examination by the club's "failure," the honestly ignorant Mrs. Roby, who stumps Dane with her introduction of the mysterious and elusive "Xingu": " 'we really can't let you off from telling us exactly what you think about Xingu; especially,' she added, with a still more persuasive smile, 'as some people say that one of your last books was saturated with it'" (218). Both Osric Dane and the club members, having no idea whatsoever what "Xingu" is, continue in a discussion of its merits and values, perfectly convinced that they know what it is. The ignorant Mrs. Roby, ironically, becomes the true artist, the "muse" whose cry of 'Xingu' is the song which "wins the singing contest over the meaningless chatter of women" (Waid 201). Wharton is pointed in her criticism of both the ladies of the club, and its celebrated guest author, markedly suggesting that they, in their ignorant pretensions to high culture, actually exist in "a region inhabited by tribes still in the Stone age of culture," just as the River Xingu in Brazil does (226).

And even as American idealism eroded into sentimentality, so too romanticism slid into sensationalism, taking the form of the dime novel, pulp fiction westerns, crime, adventure and love stories sinking the novel into what Wharton calls "the mob of irresponsible criminals" (336, *BG* 127). When *The Touchstone* (1900) was renamed for English publication as "A Gift from the Grave," Wharton sardonically comments upon its sensational and sentimental potential:

> This seductive but misleading label must have been exactly to the taste. Of the sentimental novel-reader of the day, for to my mingled wrath and amusement the book sold rapidly in England and I have often chuckled to think how defrauded the purchasers must have felt themselves after reading the first few pages. (*BG* 126)

Wharton grudgingly acknowledges here the enormous success such sensational and sentimental fiction was, and how insatiable the taste for it, for *The Touchstone*, as it was published in America, did not do nearly as well there (126). And later, when Gertrude Lane, editor of *Woman's Home Companion*, rejected her short story "Duration" in the Spring of 1933, Wharton noted that "it was beyond her 'capacity,' she said, to 'write down to the 'present standard' of the American pictorials: 'If I could turn out a series of pot-boilers for magazine consumption I should be only too glad to do so; but I really have difficulty imagining what they want'" (Benstock 439).

Another aspect of popular fiction that Wharton, claiming Darwin as one of her intellectual "awakeners," must have found distressing is the influence of the pseudo-sciences on the popular novel, such as phrenology, Christian perfectionism, animal magnetism, mesmerism, and spiritualism (Stovall 336). Wharton frequently satirizes the popularizing, and therefore oversimplifying, of scientific theory in her short fiction. We catch a glimpse of this in "The Line of Least Resistance," when the hapless Mindon ruminates on his wife's and daughters' habitual lateness as a theory of "hereditary unpunctuality." In "The Angel at the Grave" Wharton frequently references Paulina Anson's sense of predestination in devoting her life to the memory of her illustrious grandfather, satirizing Darwinian social theories. Furthermore, her grandfather, the renowned popular philosopher, was really a scientist and medical doctor whose "real work" on the *amphioxus* — "'It's an animal, isn't it – a fish?'"— has all but been forgotten or lost. Yet Paulina has devoted her life to her grandfather's "glory. . . as the chief 'authority' on the great man," entirely mistaking his greatness for the most of her life, which she spends helping "historians who were 'getting up' the period," "ladies with inexplicable yearnings" who "begged for an interpretation of phrases which had 'influenced' them, but which they had not quite understood," and "critics" who "applied to her to verify some doubtful citation or to decide some disputed point in chronology" (248). But she learns belatedly that "the great tide of thought and investigation" which "kept up a continuous murmur on the quiet shores of her life" has, according to the scholar Corby, missed the point: "'He simply leads the field! You'll help me go to the bottom of this, won't you? We must turn out all the papers – letters, journals, memoranda. He must have made notes. He must have left some record of what led up to this . . . do you know you're the granddaughter of a Great Man?" (257). The popularizing and sentimentalizing of Anson's "philosophy" and very life has, in fact destroyed his granddaughter's life, by misplacing or misunderstanding the worth of his real work in pure, not popularized, science.

Wharton explores a similar theme in "The Descent of Man," in which Professor Linyard, who scoffs at an unlettered public who "read scientific books and expressed an opinion on them" nonetheless caters his own book, *The Vital Thing*, intended to be a satire on popular fiction only appreciable to true scientists, to the very public he eschews because the financial return is too lucrative to pass up (Wharton 349). The entire story, in fact, satirizes the success of popular fiction in general: his publisher "looked as if he had been fattened on popular fiction" (351); he jokingly accuses Linyard, to the latter's distress, of causing a "sensation" with his book, and of having "such a lot of sentiment in him" (353, 357). That "ladies and the clergy had taken up" popular science galls Professor Linyard (349); that it had "passed to the schoolroom and the kindergarten" appalls him: "Daily life was regulated on scientific principles; the daily papers had their 'Scientific Jottings'; nurses passed examinations in hygienic science, and babies were fed and dandled according to the new psychology" (349). Despising America's taste for pseudo-science, melodrama and sighing sentimental piety, or "ephemeral rubbish," as she calls it in her autobiography, Wharton dislikes the sentimental and sensational not only for their own inherent lack of aesthetic value, but for the ever-increasing hunger for such writing the promulgation of these novels creates, and for the novelists who feed that hunger. Thus Linyard, who "cultivat[es] the success which accident bestowed upon him" because it "enabled him to command a greater range of appliances for his real work," becomes entirely dependent upon the subsequent monetary rewards, and must put off the continuing of his "real" work on beetles to publish a second volume of *The Vital Thing,* and quickly, because, as his publisher warns him (while writing the advance check) "popularity don't keep, you know; and the hotter the success the quicker the commodity perishes" (362).

There is, perhaps, another reason why Wharton rejects the sentimental novel: for not only did Wharton's mother deny her access to these "lesser novelists of the day" by carefully monitored her reading, but, hypocritically, they were the very "stacks of novels" that "she, my aunts and my grandmother annually devoured" (*BG* 66, 68). To reject them is, indirectly, a counter-rejection of a mother who rejected her writing career almost at its inception:

> My first attempt (at the age of eleven) was a novel, which began: 'Oh, how do you do, Mrs. Brown?' said Mrs. Tompkins. 'If only I had known you were going to call I should have tidied up the drawing-room.' Timorously I submitted this to my mother, and never shall I forget the sudden drop of my creative frenzy when she returned it with the icy comment: 'Drawing-rooms are always tidy.' (*BG* 73)

Indeed, her writing of *Fast and Loose* just a few years later seems to be a gentle mockery of the sentimental form itself; by secretly writing and "reviewing" it, Wharton proves to herself, if not to her mother, that she was capable of writing fiction that was at least as good as that which her mother was reading (11). Constantly battling identification with this kind of fiction, or with that of the local colorists, Wharton wanted her writing to be taken seriously as good art, not to be trivialized or diminished. Thus the "pastel" "taint of the sentimental and the sensational in literature is something that Wharton actively sought to avoid, never herself wanting to be labeled a "scribbling woman" of the Mrs. E.D.E.N Southworth variety, nor to have herself and her writing "classed . . . with that of other 'rich women" whose writing was merely a "'fad,'"[1] a la Osric Dane (Waid 8; Benstock 117).

Contemporary writer Jane Smiley in a National Public Radio interview defined irony as "the distance between the ideal and the real." [2] When considering

---

[1] *Munsey's Magazine*'s review of *Crucial Instances* was less than enthusiastic.

[2] Jane Smiley, in a Diane Rheim interview on National Public Radio, May 4, 2000.

Wharton's literary stance this seems a useful definition: she rejects sentimental idealism, but does not entirely embrace literary realism either. Though not aligned directly with William Dean Howells' realist movement, nor with Norris' brand of Naturalism, Wharton's approach to the world was essentially realistic – what Candace Waid calls a realism of "opposition" rather than identification (176).

"My exclusive interest as a novelist," she emphasizes in *A Backward Glance*, is "in the life about me" (156). But it is irony that provided her the means to point out the distances or discrepancies between reality and those who evade, ignore or gild it; irony allowed Wharton to demystify the real social issues and human behaviors, however inconsistent or amoral, that the sentimental novel overlooks and to explore genuine emotions, rather than bathos, in all of their depth and complexity. Irony thus becomes for Wharton the trope of her distinction: recognizing "painfully irresolvable contradictions" and "recalcitrant ironies" inherent in American social life creates a hallmark of her own unique art, the means by which she creates a continuity between her literary past and present – it is the "difference" of her "genius" (Barrish 136):

> I believe the initial mistake of most of the younger novelists,
> especially in England and America, has been the decision that the
> old forms were incapable of producing new ones. No work based
> on the determination to be different seems to have a principle of
> life in it; genius is always 'different' (that is, individual) in spite of
> itself; but never merely for the sake of being so" ("Tendencies in
> Modern Fiction" 170).

Perhaps, then, the most covert, infinitely unstable of all of Wharton's ironies in her short fiction rests in its very use. Discussing in *A Backward Glance* the dramatist Clyde Fitch, who adapted *House of Mirth* for the stage, Wharton defines her own sense of irony, remarking that although "his sense of the theatre was keen,....that interested me no less than his sense of the irony of life, his happy choice of the incidents by means of which he threw light on the human predicament" (161). For while irony is for Wharton a trope of distinction, difference, exclusion from the mob of sentimental and popular fiction writers, it is also paradoxically and simultaneously, a trope of *inclusiveness,* as Phillip Barrish argues, a trope which throws light on one human predicament, the need for belonging: social, physical, and intellectual (Barrish 127). Wharton's own need for and lack of artistic approval, and her need for intellectual companionship began early in her childhood. Wharton describes herself as an "omnivorous" reader, whose favorite pastime was vigorous and solitary bouts of "making-up," telling, and pretending to write stories (*BG* 65). Biographer Shari Benstock argues that Wharton's reaction to language and literature was sensual, quasi-orgasmic: "her desire for language – whether Holy Writ, Renaissance sonnets, or everyday vernacular – transgressed the boundaries of convention – as though, as Helen Killoran convincingly suggests, she was driven by the furies themselves in her voracious need for intellectual interactions (*Edith Wharton: Art and Illusion* 190). Even at this early age, she was pulled between conforming to social codes and giving free reign to her powers of expression (Benstock 21). But Wharton was educated spottily, depending on governesses, and friends such as Emlyn Washburn and Emlyn's father (cousin to Ralph Waldo Emerson, and a member of the Boston Transcendentalists) rather than the formal private school education in classics, philosophy, math and the sciences that her brothers received, to fill in the gaps as best they could (33). Wharton became her own teacher, relying primarily on her father's library, to which she had full access; her father himself seems largely absent as an intellectual role model. Benstock speculates that there was, from Wharton's recollections of him, something sad, or missing, or diminished about him, due perhaps to an intellectual mismatch with Lucretia, whose earlier fondness for sentimental Victorian verse may have convinced him that "his beloved apparently had no poetry in her soul" (22).

Further alienating Wharton intellectually is her parents' attitude towards writers in general: "authorship was still regarded," Wharton tells us, "as something between a black art and a form of manual labor," both eschewed by the moneyed, conservative and indolent Old New York society (*BG* 67-68). This set of Old New Yorkers deemed the contemporaneous Washington Irving and Longfellow acceptable despite their literary popularity because they were "gentlemen" (*BG* 67-68). But Melville, though by birth a cousin to the Van Rensselaers, and therefore certainly of gentlemanly status, was too "bohemian" (68); Poe was "drunken and demoralized," the journalist Fitz James O'Brien and novelists Joseph Drake and Harriet Beecher Stowe were too "common" (68).

In addition, Wharton's own friends were "kindly" but "frivolous," completely unsympathetic to her "secret dreams" of becoming a serious writer (68). She remembers, sadly, that she "could not believe that a girl like myself could ever write anything worth reading, and my friends would certainly have agreed with me" (88). For years Wharton lacked any kind of intellectual companionship, or even a sympathetic ear to which she might whisper her ambitions, and have them respected. Indeed, even after years of literary success, her New York friends and family remained "puzzled and embarrassed" by her acclaim, and not only never encouraged her to continue with her writing, but never acknowledged her as a successful writer (143-144). With the exception of one "eccentric widowed cousin" none of her family "ever spoke" of her writing "either to praise or to blame, seeing it as a "kind of family disgrace, which might be condoned but could not be forgotten" (143-144). Beneath her rather matter-of-fact recollections, Wharton understandably sounds a bitter note about her family's attitude towards her career: "I had to fight my way to expression through a thick fog of indifference, if not of tacit disapproval" (122). Irony thus allows Wharton a safe, covert means of revealing her opinions without receiving the disapprobation of family and friends (Singley, "Edith Wharton's Ironic Realism 228).

Finally, Wharton's intellectual isolation is exacerbated by her unhappy marriage to Teddy Wharton. Not unlike her parents' relationship, hers with Teddy is one of intellectual unequals. In her autobiography Wharton describes Teddy in rare, sketchy references as pleasant and outdoorsy, sharing merely her love for dogs and travel; she seems to have felt a lukewarm affection for him at best (Benstock 60). She had few close female friends early in her marriage with whom to commiserate, and neither great emotion nor great physical passion from her marriage: "rather than bringing her into the magic circle of feminine self-knowledge, marriage isolated her from women" as well (60).

Existing thus on an intellectual plain remote from those who hitherto have peopled her life, Wharton only achieved personal intellectual kinship by achieving literary success – neither her family, her society friends, nor her marriage serve but to isolate her. She thus reinvents her family by cultivating her "inner group" of friends, intellectuals, scholars, writers, and critics all, including Paul and Minnie Bourget, Henry James, Howard Sturgis, Walter Berry, Bay Lodge, Robert Norton, Gaillard Lapsley and John-Hugh Smith (192). She finds "joy" in their "rarest understanding, the richest and most varied mental comradeship" for which she had been longing for almost thirty years (*BG* 169). Though many have argued tritely the importance of Henry James as a literary role model in Wharton's artistic development, citing her similarity with him in theme and style, James' importance to Wharton rests not only in what he wrote, but what he was to Wharton. In *A Backward Glance* she warmly recalls his "silver-footed ironies," his conversation, "the whole so sunned over by irony, sympathy and wide-flashing fun" (not to mention the occasional malice) that only members of the inner group would catch and understand (178):

> an almost immediate sympathy had established itself between the various members, so that our common stock of allusions, cross-references, pleasantries was always increasing, and new waves of interest in the same book or picture, or any sort of dramatic event in life or letters, would simultaneously flood through our minds. (192)

Henry James, large physically when Wharton entered his coterie, is larger than life in his discursive speech as well; he is a metonymy for the group itself, and for Wharton's joy in becoming an "initiate," by successfully interpreting its ironies

(178). To Wharton, the ultimate sympathy between two people, "the real marriage of true minds," is "a sense of humor or irony pitched in exactly the same key, so that their joint glances at any subject cross like interarching search-lights" (*BG* 173). She therefore emotionally can discard her legal marriage in favor of an intellectual one, irony figuring both as the language with which each spouse speaks, and as the offspring of their relationship, the process and the product. Irony in her short fiction provides Wharton with the appropriate emotional distance with which to examine and illuminate the emotionally charged human predicaments of the human need for intellectual and emotional companionship, and the fear of its loss, by becoming the trope of her own need and fear of loss.

Wharton's heavily ironized "marriage question" stories, for example, all incorporate this theme of the need for social and personal inclusion; the degree of irony present signals the degree to which significant human relationships will be possible for her characters, and contributes to the degree of sympathy we feel towards them as well. As Lydia in "Souls Belated" becomes all the more ironic, she also becomes all the more authentic in her need to fit into a social niche, even as she hypocritically feigns marriage, sacrificing her unconventional ideals to do so. Paulina Trant in "The Long Run" has found in Merrick a soul-mate not unlike the one Wharton herself found in Morton Fullerton: Merrick and Paulina share both an intellectual and emotional connection. But we sympathize all the more with Paulina because we see this love unfulfilled, through the irony of its loss. In "The Reckoning" Julia Westall is forced to admit that the doctrine of self-freedom upon which she has based her marriage does not account for her human need to be loved. It is only when under the bright light of irony that she not only sees that her husband does not love her any longer, but also that, sadly, she does love him. And in "Autres Temps . . ." Mrs. Lidcote's social isolation from friends and family echoes Wharton's own early feelings. Through the irony of society's refusal to readmit her despite its change in values, through the irony of her own daughter's similar marital status that should, but does not singularly equip her to welcome her mother into the new New York, and through the irony of Franklin Ide's hypocrisy in wanting to become her soul-mate, but only if they can be together away from New York, can we truly feel the endless depths of Mrs. Lidcote's loss and appreciate how utterly alone in the world she is.

Another such character appears in the little-treated story "Confession." We meet Kate "Ingram," a.k.a. Kate Spain, through the innocent eyes of Severance, recuperating in the same hotel in the Alps as she. He notices something unusual and incongruous about her and her traveling companion Cassie Wilpert immediately – Kate appears refined, old-fashioned, yet subservient to the fashionable but coarse Cassie. Kate is an enigma, "different . . . a little uncertain and ill at ease in the ordinary scene, but at home and sure of herself elsewhere. Where?" (803). Falling in love with her almost upon first sight, he then learns from an acquaintance, newspaperman Jimmy Shreve, of a violent past: her abusive father had been murdered, and she had been tried and acquitted on the basis of her maid's testimony. Discovering shortly before her death that Kate's demanding traveling companion Cassie is really that very same maid, Severance ultimately convinces her to marry him, but only after receiving a confessional letter whose seal he never breaks. This plot of the story reads like those Wharton herself derided; it is romantic, with a sentimental relationship between the two characters, and sensational details looming in the background. Even Severance himself is aware of the ludicrously over-sentimental and over-sensational situation he finds himself in, trying to convince himself that his feelings are somehow more authentic:

> From the first I had tried to explain away my passion by regarding it as the idle man's tendency to fall into sentimental traps; but I had always known that what I felt was not of that nature. This quiet woman with the wide pale eyes and melancholy mouth had taken possession of me; she seemed always to have inhabited my mind and heart. (815)

Jimmy Shreve, too conveniently arriving on the scene to provide him with the necessary but lurid background information as to her past and identity, represents in his "craving for the sensational [that] had certainly deformed his critical faculty" the standard American reader, who would certainly love such a tale (815).

What keeps this tale from slipping into sentimental melodrama is the irony with which Wharton treats Severance's feelings for Kate. Rather than feeling horror at Shreve's insinuation that the woman Severance thinks he loves is a murderess, he looks at it altogether differently. Upon declaring his love for her his first thoughts were not merely on the mystery of her past; "all sorts of unsought problems instantly crowded out my sentimental musings" (815). He wonders, "Who is she? What, in short, did I know of her? . . . .Was she married? Unmarried, divorced, a widow? Had she children, parents, relations, distant or near? (815). He senses her existence on the outskirts of society; the people who might identify her, and therefore place her within it are not there – she is entirely alone. Severance genuinely empathizes with her solitary state, and his love for her is in some measure a means of saving her from the fate of loneliness. Did Kate really kill her father? Did Cassie's death prove that she did, because she was responsible for that too? Wharton never leads us down a suspenseful path towards the true answers to these queries. We see, oddly, the irony of a man's falling in love with a stranger, feeling intimate with her because of her very strangeness and lack of intimates in her own life. We also see irony in his finding his soul-mate in the very least likely, least socially acceptable person – the ultimate social pariah. And there is irony too in having the truth available, but never accessing it. Severance simply chooses love, companionship, a sense of belonging and fitness with Kate, over truth, or, for that matter, over moral rectitude, refusing to turn their relationship into a question of ethics, morals or principles despite the obvious moral problem of marrying a woman who may be a murderess twice over. This is hugely ironic in a tale whose plot would suggest a much different outcome, including the sensational unfolding of violent details, and loud declarations of undying "love conquers all" from both the hero and heroine.

Strangely, this rather quiet and dignified, if somewhat mediocre little tale ends as no other Wharton story does, culminating in a happy marriage: "for five years we lived our strange perilous dream of happiness" (832). Also peculiar is that Kate is one of the few Wharton characters who does, at least temporarily, escape or overcome or ignore her past in a way that Charlotte Ashby or Mrs. Lidcote never could: "She did not dream, at first, that it [the confessional letter] had given me a complete insight into her character and that that was all I wanted of it . . . I was determined to judge her, not by her past, whatever it might have been, but by what she had unconsciously revealed of herself since I had known and loved her" (832).What redeems the story somewhat from the "better to have loved and lost" cliché is, ironically, that their happiness is fleeting and "perilous," not allowing Kate to go entirely untouched by a past that is, at the very least, troubled. Unusually, and therefore significantly, these characters make a bid for love without being overly sentimental; Severance, in avoiding the truth of Kate's past, refuses to be overwhelmed by the sensationalism of it. One senses Wharton's "bravo" that these two characters, unlike others in her short story canon, were courageous enough to seize the relationship in front of them, to allow themselves to exist together in a present that is "blind with remembered joy," despite the societal disapprobation they could expect, and without letting their fear of inevitable "sorrow," either of the past or the future, keep them from acting at all, and thus keep them apart (832).

Wharton critiques popular taste and the popular novel as she invokes them in her short stories, showing us her view of the state of American intellectual life and letters. She consciously uses irony as a means of distinguishing herself from the "scribbling" popular novelists who precede her, and to portray herself as a writer who has never ceased to be in touch with the human need for social, emotional, and intellectual attachments. Her best stories especially end in ambiguity, not resolution, and the irony generated from this ambiguity, from the leaving of paradoxes unresolved, is the most covert, infinite and unstable irony – but the more difficulty we have in reading her ironies, the closer we are to Wharton the woman, as though in gaining ironic understanding, we too can be admitted to her inner circle. Edith Wharton defies labels, creating for herself a unique niche in American Letters. Edith Wharton's ironic stance gives her individuality as an artist, and provides her art with its vitality, wit and validity that made her a valuable writer in the previous century, and will continue to do so into the next.

Bibliography

Published Short Stories
Abbreviations following first publication statement indicate the short story collections, listed below, in which they next appeared.

"The Angel at the Grave." *Scribner's Magazine* 29 (February 1901):158-166. *DM*
"Autres Temps . . ." (as "Other Times, Other Manners.") *The Century Magazine* 82 (July 1911):344-352. *X*
"The Descent of Man." *Scribner's Magazine* 35 (March 1904): 313-322. *DM*
"Confession." (as "Unconfessed Crimes") *Storyteller* 58 (March 1936):64-85. *WO*
"The Lamp of Psyche." *Scribner's Magazine* 18 (October 1895):418-428.
"The Last Asset." *Scaribner's Magazine* 36 (August 1904): 150-168. *HWW*
"The Line of Least Resistance." *Lippincott's 66* (October 1900): 559-570.
"The Long Run." *Atlantic Monthly* 109 (February 1912): 145-63. *X*
"Mrs. Manstey's View." *Scribner's Magazine* 10 (July 1891): 117-22.
"The Muse's Tragedy." *Scribner's Magazine* 25 (January 1899): 77-84. *GI*
"The Other Two." *Collier's* 32 (13 February 1904): 15. *DM*
"Pomegranate Seed." *Saturday Evening Post* 203 (25 April 1931):6. *WO*
"The Reckoning." *Harper's Magazine* 105 (August 1902):342-355. *DM*
"Souls Belated." *The Greater Inclination.* New York: Scribner's, 1899.
"The Temperate Zone." *Pictoral Review* 25 (February 1924): 5. *HB*
"Xingu." *Scribner's Magazine* 50 (December 1911):683-696. *X*

Short Story Collections

The Best Short Stories of Edith Wharton. New York: Scribner's, 1958.
Certain People. New York: Appleton, 1930.
The Collected Short Stories. Ed. R.W.B. Lewis. New York: Charles Scribner's Sons, 1968. 2 vols.
The Collected Stories of Edith Wharton. Introd. Anita Brookner. NY: Carroll & Graf Publishers, Inc., 1998.
Crucial Instances. New York: Scribner's, 1901. *CI*
The Descent of Man and Other Stories. New York: Scribner's, 1904. *DM*
The Ghost Stories of Edith Wharton. New York: Scribner's, 1973. Rpt. New York: Popular Library, 1976.
Ghosts. New York: Appleton-Century, 1937.
The Greater Inclination. New York: Scribner's, 1899. *GI*
Here and Beyond. New York: Appleton, 1926. *HB*
The Hermit and the Wild Woman and Other Stories. New York: Scribner's, 1908. *HWW*
Human Nature. New York: Appleton, 1933.
Madame de Treymes and Other Stories. New York: Scribner's, 1907.

The Muse's Tragedy and Other Stories. Ed. Candace Waid. New York: New
American Library, 1990.
Quartet. Kentfield, CA: Allen Press, 1975.
Roman Fever and Other Stories. Ed. Cynthia Griffin Wolff. New York:
Collier Books, 1987.
The Stories of Edith Wharton. Introd. Anita Brookner. 1988. 2 vols.
Tales of Men and Ghosts. New York: Scribner's, 1910.
The World Over. New York: Appleton, 1936. *WO*
Xingu and Other Stories. New York: Scribner's, 1916. *X*

Other Published Primary Sources
The Age of Innocence. Introd. R.W.B. Lewis. New York: Scribner's, 1970.
Artemis to Actaeon and Other Verse. New York: Scribner's, 1909.
A Backward Glance. 1934. New York: Charles Scribner's Sons, 1964.
"Beatrice Palmato." *Edith Wharton: A Biography*. By R.W. B. Louis. New York:
Harper, 1986. 548-48.
The Buccaneers. New York: Appleton-Century, 1938.
The Children. New York: Appleton, 1928.
The Custom of the Country. Introd. Marilyn French. New York: Berkeley, 1981.
The Decoration of Houses. New York: Scribner's, 1897.
Edith Wharton Abroad: Selected Travel Writings, 1888-1920. Ed. Sara Bird
Wright. New York: St. Martin's Griffin, 1995.
Edith Wharton: Novellas and other Writings. Ed. Cynthia Griffin Wolff. New
York: Library of America, 1990.
Ethan Frome. New York: Scribner's, 1911.
Fast and Loose: A Novelette by David Olivery (Juvenalia, c. 1870) Ed. Viola
Hopkins Winner. Charlote, VA: University Press of Virginia, 1977.
"Fiction and Criticism." *The Uncollected Critical Writings* .Ed. Frederick
Wegener. Princeton: Princeton University Press, 1996
French Ways and their Meanings. New York: Appleton, 1919.
The Fruit of the Tree. New York: Scribner's, 1907
The Glimpses of the Moon. New York: Appleton, 1922.
The Gods Arrive. New York: Appleton, 1932.
The House of Mirth. New York: Scribner's, 1905.
Hudson River Bracketed. New York: Appleton, 1929.
In Morocco. New York: Scribner's, 1920.
Italian Backgrounds. New York: Scribner's, 1905.
Italian Villas and Their Gardens. New York: Century, 1904.
The Letters of Edith Wharton. Ed. R.W.B. Lewis and Nancy Lewis. New York:
Scribner's, 1988.
"Life and I." *Edith Wharton: Novellas and Other Writings*. Ed. Cynthia Griffin
Wolff. New York: Library of America, 1990. 1069-96.
The Marne. New York: Appleton, 1918.

The Mother's Recompense. New York: Appleton, 1925.
A Motor-Flight Through France. London: Macmillan, 1908.
Old New York (Four Novellas). 1925. New York: Simon and Schuster's, 1995.
"Permanent Values in Fiction." *The Uncollected Critical Writings.* Ed.
    Frederick Wegener. Princeton: Princeton University Press, 1996.
The Reef. New York: Appleton, 1912.
Sanctuary. New York: Scribner's, 1903.
Summer. New York: Appleton, 1917.
"Tendencies in Modern Fiction." *The Uncollected Critical Writings.* Ed.
    Frederick Wegener. Princeton: Princeton University Press, 1996.
The Touchstone. New York: Scribner's, 1900.
Twilight Sleep. New York: Appleton, 1927.
Twelve Poems. London: Medici Society, 1926.
The Uncollected Critical Writings. Ed. Frederick Wegener. Princeton:
    Princeton University Press, 1996.
The Valley of Decision. New York: Scribner's, 1902.
"The Vice of Reading." *The Uncollected Critical Writings.* Ed. Frederick
    Wegener. Princeton: Princeton University Press, 1996.
The Writing of Fiction. 1925. New York: Simon & Schuster, 1997.

Biographies

Auchincloss, Louis. *Edith Wharton; A Woman In Her Time.* New York: Viking
    Press, 1971.
Benstock, Shari. *No Gifts From Chance: A Biography of Edith Wharton.* London:
    Hamish Hamilton, 1994.
Dwight, Eleanor. *Edith Wharton: An Extraordinary Life.* New York: Harry N.
    Abrams, Inc., 1994.
Lewis, R.W.B. *Edith Wharton: A Biography.* New York: Harper and Row
    Publishers, 1975.
Lubbock, Percy. *Portrait of Edith Wharton* New York: D. Appleton-Century,
    1947.
Wolff, Cynthia Griffin. *A Feast of Words: The Triumph of Edith Wharton.* New
    York: Oxford, 1977.

Secondary Sources

Ammons, Elizabeth. *Edith Wharton's Argument with America.* Athens: University
    of Georgia Press, 1980.
Auchincloss, Louis. *Pioneers and Caretakers; A study of Nine American Women
    Novelists.* Minneapolis, MN: University of Minnesota Press, 1965.
Balestra, Gianfranca. "For the Use of the Magazine Morons': Edith Wharton

Rewrites the Tale of the Fantastic." *Studies in Short Fiction* 33.1(Winter 1996):13-25.

Banta, Martha. "The Ghostly Gothic of Wharton's Everyday World." *American Literary Realism* 27.1(Fall 1994): 1-10.

Barrish, Phillip. *American Literary Realism, Critical Theory and Intellectual Prestige 1880-1995*. Cambridge: Cambridge University Press, 2001.

Bauer, Dale M. *Edith Wharton's Brave New Politics.* Madison: University of Wisconsin Press, 1994.

Bell, Millicent, ed. *The Cambridge Companion to Edith Wharton.* New York: Cambridge University Press, 1995.

Bentley, Nancy. *The Ethnography of Manners: Hawthorne, James, Wharton.* New York: Cambridge University Press, 1995.

Bendixen, Alfred. Introduction. *Edith Wharton: New Critical Essays.* Ed. Alfred Bendixen and Annette Zilversmit. New York: London: Garland Publishing Inc.,1992.

———. "The World of Wharton Criticism: A Bibliographic Essay." *Edith Wharton Review* 7.1 (Spring 1990):18-22.

Bloom, Harold. *Edith Wharton.* New York: Chelsea House, 1968.

Booth, Wayne C. *The Rhetoric of Irony.* Chicago: London: University of Chicago Press,1974.

Brown, Mary Margaret. "Edith Wharton's Irony: From the Short Stories to the Infinitudes." *DAI* 51 (1991): 2742A.

Caudle, David J. "Edith Wharton (1862-1937)." *American Women Writers, 1900-1945: A Bio-Bibliographical Critical Sourcebook.* Ed. Laurie Champion. Westport, CT: Greenwood Press, 2000.

Campbell, Donna M. "Edith Wharton and the 'Authoresses': The Critique of local Color in Wharton's Early Fiction." *Studies in American Fiction* 22.2 (Autumn 1994): 169-83.

Chandler, Marilyn R. *Dwelling in the Text: Houses In American Fiction.* Berkeley, CA: University of California Press, 1991.

Colquitt, Clare. "Contradictory Possibilities: Wharton Scholarship 1992-1994." *Edith Wharton Review* 12.2(Fall 1995): 37-41.

Commins, Barbara. "'Pecking at the Host': Transgressive Wharton." *Edith Wharton Review* 14.1(Spring 1997): 18-21.

Dessner, Lawrence Jay. "Edith Wharton and the Problem of Form." *Ball State University Forum* 24 (1983): 54-63.

Dyman, Jenni. *Lurking Feminism: The Ghost Stories of Edith Wharton.:* New York: Peter Lang, 1996.

Erlich, Gloria. *The Sexual Education of Edith Wharton.* Berkeley, CA: University of California Press, 1992.

Fedorko, Kathy. *Gender and the Gothic in the Fiction of Edith Wharton.* Tuscaloosa: University of Alabama Press, 1995.

———."Edith Wharton's Haunted Fiction: 'The Lady's Maid's Bell' and *The*

House of Mirth." *Haunting the House of Fiction: Feminist Perspectives on Ghost Stories by American Women.* Ed. Lynette Carpenter and Wendy K. Kolmar. Knoxville, TN: University of Tennessee Press, 1991.

Flynn, Dale Bachman. "salamanders in the Fire: the Short Stories of Edith Wharton." *DAI* 45 (1985): 3638A

Fracasso, Evelyn E. *Edith Wharton's Prisoners of Consciousness.* Westport: London: Greenwood Press, 1994.

Fryer, Judith. "Edith Wharton." *American Women Fiction Writers 1900-1960.* Vol.3. Ed. Harold Bloom. Philadelphia, PA: Chelsea House, 1997.

Goodman, Susan. *Edith Wharton's Women: Friends and Rivals.* Hanover, NH: University Press of New England, 1990.

Goodwynn, Janet Beer. *Edith Wharton: Traveller in the Land of Letters.* London: Macmillan Press, 1990.

Hadley, Katherine Miller. *In the Interstices of the Tale: Edith Wharton's Narrative Strategies.* New York: Peter Lang, 1993.

——."Ironic Structure and Untold Stories in *the Age of Innocence.*" *Studies in the Novel.* 23.2 (Summer 1991): 262-271.

Handwerk, Gary. *Irony and Ethics in Narrative: From Schlegel to Lacan.* New Haven: Yale University Press, 1985.

Heller, Janet Ruth. "Ghosts and Marital Estrangement: An Analysis of 'Afterward.'" *Edith Wharton Review* 10.1(Spring 1993): 18-19.

Hoeller, Hildegarde. *Edith Wharton's Dialogue with Realism and Sentimental Fiction.* Gainsville: University Press of Florida, 2000.

Howard, June. *Form and History in American Literary Naturalism.* Chapel Hill: London: University of North Carolina Press, 1985.

Howe, Irving, ed. *Edith Wharton: A Collection of Critical Essays.* Englewood Cliffs, NJ: Prentice Hall, 1962.

Iness, Sherrie A. "An Economy of Beauty: The Beauty System in 'The Looking Glass' and 'Permanent Wave.'" *Edith Wharton Review* 10.1(Spring 1993): 7-11.

Joslin, Katherine. "Edith Wharton and the Critics." *Women Writers: Edith Wharton.* New York: St. Martin's Press, 1991. 128-50.

Kellogg, Grace. *The Two Lives of Edith Wharton: the Woman and her Work.* New York: Appleton, 1965.

Kaye, Richard A. "Textual Hermeneutics and Belated Male Heroism: Edith Wharton's Revisions of *The House of Mirth* and the Resistance to American Literary Naturalism." *Arizona Quarterly* 52.3(Autumn 1995): 87-116.

Killoran, Helen. *The Critical Reception of Edith Wharton.* Rochester: Camden House, 2001.

——. *Edith Wharton: Art and Allusion.* Tuscaloosa: London: University of Alabama Press, 1996.

——. "Pascal, Brönte, and 'Kerfol': The Horrors of a Foolish Quarrel"

168

(misprinted as 'Quartet') *Edith Wharton Review* 10.1(Spring 1993): 12-17.
———. "Sexuality and Abnormal Psychology in Edith Wharton's 'The Lady's Maid's Bell.'" *CEA Critic* 58.3(Spring-Summer 1996): 41-49.
Kronenberger, Louis. "Mrs. Wharton's Literary Museum." *Atlantic Monthly* 222 (September 1968): 7-19.
Lauer, Kristin O. and Margaret P. Murray. *Edith Wharton: An Annotated Secondary Bibliography.* New York: London: Garland Publishing, Inc., 1990.
The Letters of Edith Wharton. Ed. R.W.B. Lewis and Nancy Lewis. New York: Macmillan Publishing Company, 1988.
Lewis, R. W. B. "A Writer of Short Stories." *Modern Critical Views: Edith Wharton* Ed. Harold Bloom. New York: Chelsea House, 1986.
———. Introduction. *The Collected Short Stories.* By Edith Wharton. Ed. R.W. B. Lewis. Vol.1.New York: Charles Scribner's Sons, 1968. 2 vols.
McDowell, Margaret. *Edith Wharton.* Boston: Twayne Publishers, 1976.
———. "Edith Wharton's Ghost Tales Reconsidered." *Edith Wharton: New Critical Essays.* Eds.Alfred Bendixen and Annette Zilversmit. New York: Garland, 1992.
Merrish, Lori. "Engendering Naturalism: Narrative Form and Commodity Spectacle in U.S. Naturalist Fiction." *Novel: A Forum on Fiction.* 29.3(Spring 1996):319-45.
Miller, Carol. " 'Natural Magic': Irony as Unifying Strategy in *The House of Mirth.*" *South Central Review.* 4 (1987): 82-91.
Muecke, D. C. *The Compass of Irony.* London: Methuen and Co., Ltd., 1969.
Nettels, Elsa. "Gender and First Person Narration in Edith Wharton's Short Fiction." *Edith Wharton: New Critical Essays.* Ed. Alfred Bendixen and Annette Zilversmit. New York: London: Garland Publishing Inc., 1992.
———. *Language and Gender in American Fiction: Howells, James, Wharton and Cather.* Charlottesville, VA: University Press of Virginia, 1997.
———. "Wharton and Cather." *American Literary Scholarship: an Annual* (2000) 113-127.
Newlin, Maureen C. "Edith Wharton's Irony" Marginalizations and the 'Submerged' Narrator's Point of View." *DAI* 60:9(2000 March), 3364.
Nevius, Blake. *Edith Wharton: A Study of Her Fiction.* Berkeley: University of California, 1953.
Ong, Walter. "From Mimesis to Irony: The Distancing Voice." *The Horizon of Literature.* Ed.Paul Hernadi. Lincoln: Univeristy of Nebraska Press, 1982.
Paternoster, Anna. "Art and Identity in the Short Stories of Edith Wharton." *DAI* 60:9 (2000 March) 3364-65.
Plante, Patricia R. "Edith Wharton as a Short Story Writer.' *Midwest Quarterly* 4 (Summer 1962): 363-370.
Quinn, Arthur Hobson. *Edith Wharton.* New York: Appleton-Century, 1938.

Raphael, Lev. *Edith Wharton's Prisoners of Shame: A New Perspective on Her Neglected Fiction.* New York: St. Martin's Press, 1991.

Saunders, Judith P. "Ironic Reversal in Edith Wharton's 'Bunner Sisters.'" *Studies in Short Fiction* 14 (1977): 241-245.

Schriber, Mary Suzanne. "Darwin, Wharton and 'The Descent of Man': Blueprints of American Society." *Studies in Short Fiction* 17 (1980): 31-38.

Sensibar, Judith L. "Edith Wharton Reads the Bachelor Type: Her Critique of Modernism's Representative Man." *Edith Wharton: New Critical Essays. Edith Wharton: New Critical Essays* Ed. Alfred Bendixen and Annette Zilversmit. New York: Garland, 1992.

Singley, Carol J. "Edith Wharton's Ironic Realism." *Challenging Boundaries: Gender and Periodization.* Ed. Joyce Warren and Margarate Dickie. Athens, GA: University of Georgia Press, 2000.

———. *Edith Wharton: Matters of Mind and Spirit.* Cambridge: CambridgeUniversity Press 1995.

———."Gothic Borrowings and Invocations in Edith Wharton's 'A Bottle of Perrier." *Edith Wharton: New Critical Essays* Ed. Alfred Bendixen and Annette Zilversmit. New York: Garland, 1992.

Singley, Carol J. and Susan Elizabeth Sweeny, eds. "Forbidden Reading and Ghostly Writing in Edith Wharton's 'The Pomegranate Seed.'" *Anxious Power: Reading, Writing, and Ambivalence in Narrative by Women.* New York: State University of New York Press, 1993.

Smith, Herbert F. *The Popular American Novel 1865-1920.* Boston: Twayne Publishers, 1980.

Stange, Magrit. "Edith Wharton and the Problem of the Woman Author." *Personal Property: Wives, White Slaves, and the Market in Women.* Baltimore, MD: Johns Hopkins University Press, 1998.

Stovall, Floyd. *American Idealism.* Norman: University of Oklahoma Press, 1943.

———. "The Decline of Romantic Idealism, 1855-1871." *Transitions in American Literary History.* Ed. Harry Haden Clark. New York: Octagon books, Inc., 1967.

Sweeny, Susan Elizabeth. "Mirror, Mirror, On the Wall: Gazing in Edith Wharton's 'Looking Glass.'" *Narrative* 3.2 (May 1995): 139-60.

Thomas, Jennice G. "Spook or Spinster? Edith Wharton's 'Miss Mary Pask.'" *Haunting the House of Fiction: Feminist Perspectives on Ghost Stories by American Women.* Eds. Lynette Carpenter and Wendy K. Kolmar. Knoxville, TN: University of Tennessee Press, 1991.

Tuttleton, James W., Kristin O. Lauer, and Margaret P. Murray, eds. *Edith Wharton: The Contemporary Reviews.* New York: Cambridge University Press, 1992.

Vita-Finzi, Penelope. *Edith Wharton and the Art of Fiction.* New York: St. Martin's Press, 1990.

Waid, Candace. *Edith Wharton's Letters from the Underworld: Fictions of Women and Writing.* Chapel Hill: London: University of North Carolina Press, 1991.

Wagner-Martin, Linda. "Prospects for the Study of Edith Wharton." *Resources for American Literary Studies* 22.1(1996): 1-5.

Wilson-Jordan, Jacqueline S. "Telling the Story that Can't Be Told: Hartley's Role as Dis-Eased Narrator in 'The Lady's Maid's Bell.'" *Edith Wharton Review* 14.1(Spring 1997): 12-17, 21.

White, Barbara A. *Edith Wharton: A Study of the Short Fiction.* New York: Twayne Publishers, 1991.

Wiser, William. *The Great Good Place: American Expatriate Women in Paris.* New York: Norton and Co., 1991.

Witzig, M. Denise. "'The Muse's Tragedy' and The Muse's Text: Language and Desire in Edith Wharton." *Edith Wharton: New Critical Essays.* Ed. Alfred Bendixen and Annette Zilversmit. New York: London: Garland Publishing, Inc., 1992.

Wolff, Cynthia Griffin. Introduction. *Roman Fever and Other Stories.* By Edith Wharton. New York: Collier Books, 1987.

Young, Judy. "The Repudiation of Sisterhood in Edith Wharton's 'Pomegranate Seed.'" *Studies in Short Fiction* 33(1996): 1-11.

Zilversmit, Annette. "All Souls': Wharton's Last Haunted House and Future Directions for Criticism." *Edith Wharton: New Critical Essays* Ed. Alfred Bendixen and Annette Zilversmit. New York: Garland, 1992.

——. "Edith Wharton's Last Ghosts." *College Literature* 14 (1987): 296-309.

The children's view of self was frequently self-deprecating, however there were also positive self-views. Expressions reflecting a negative self-view were often that they 'hated' themselves, thought that they were 'dumb' and 'stupid', and believed that they were a 'whimp.' Sarcasm was often used during self-deprecating comments. The children would state something positive about themselves, and the statement would be followed by 'Not!' On two nights, 'opposite day' was declared by one child, which meant that everything that was said was the opposite of what they felt or believed. The positive self-views were expressed through the children's skills and abilities, such as sports or arts, 'cool clothes,'

PS 3545 .H 16

PS 3545 H16 Z593

PS 3545 H16 Z8786

PS 3545 H16 Z636
1992?

Index